GW00538461

Touring Car
1998-1999 year

Touring Car
1998-1999 year

CONTENTS

THE OFFICIAL REVIEW OF THE AUTOTRADER RAC TOURING CAR CHAMPIONSHIP 1998
EDITOR SIMON STRANG **ASSISTANT EDITOR** NICK PHILLIPS **ART EDITOR** TERRY HAWES
CONTRIBUTORS MARK SKEWIS, MARCUS SIMMONS, JONATHAN NOBLE, CHARLES
BRADLEY, BRUCE JONES **PHOTOGRAPHY** LAT, BOTHWELL PHOTOGRAPHIC,
ADDITIONAL PHOTOGRAPHY MALCOLM GRIFFITHS, PETER FOX,
SHUTTERSPEED, SUTTON MOTORSPORT IMAGES
ASSOCIATE EDITOR ANDY HALLBERY **ART DIRECTOR** PETER CHARLES
PUBLISHER MARTIN NOTT **PUBLISHING MANAGER** JULIAN DANIELS
SALES DIRECTOR JOHN CHAMBERS **PUBLISHING DIRECTORS** PETER FOUBISTER,
JEREMY VAUGHAN **MANAGING DIRECTOR** TONY SCHULP

TOURING CAR YEAR 1998-1999 IS AN AUTOSPORT SPECIAL PROJECT PUBLISHED
BY HAYMARKET SPECIALIST PUBLICATIONS LTD, 38-42 HAMPTON ROAD,
TEDDINGTON, MIDDX TW11 0JE ENGLAND. TEL: 0181 943 5000 FAX: 0181 943 5079
PRODUCTION MANAGER JIM TURNER
COLOUR ORIGINATION BY: COLOUR SYSTEMS, LONDON
PRINTED IN ENGLAND BY: HUBBARD PRINT, SHEFFIELD
A HAYMARKET PUBLICATION REPRINTING IN WHOLE OR IN PART IS FORBIDDEN EXCEPT WITH PRIOR
PERMISSION OF THE PUBLISHER. FIRST PUBLISHED 1998. ISBN 0-86024-928-X
© COPYRIGHT HAYMARKET SPECIALIST PUBLICATIONS 1998
THE AUTOTRADER RAC TOURING CAR CHAMPIONSHIP IS ORGANISED BY TOCA LTD, THE MANOR, HASELEY
BUSINESS CENTRE, WARWICK CV35 7LS. TEL: 01203 537037 FAX: 01203 537038

Moving up a gear

Alan Gow - TOCA

I'd like to think 1998 will be remembered as the year when we moved the Auto Trader British Touring Car Championship onto an even higher plain.

The object behind the introduction of One-Shot Showdown qualifying procedures for a new shorter Sprint Race plus mandatory pit stops during an extended Feature Race was to produce more unpredictability. Together they helped to produce a record nine different race winners and a memorable title race, which went right down to the wire.

Crucially these new formats also found favour with the drivers, teams and most importantly the fans.

No doubt boosted by the added attraction of Nigel Mansell, we had record crowds at Brands Hatch and Silverstone. More people than ever followed the BTCC on television too, thanks to our landmark deal to screen the championship in China, the world's largest market.

And, rest assured, there are more innovations in the pipeline. Indeed we have already announced the addition of a spectacular night-racing meeting in 1999.

I hope you enjoy re-living all the thrills of last season's BTCC in the pages of this book and can assure you next year's championship will once again be one to savour.

PETER J FOX

VOLVO

Q8

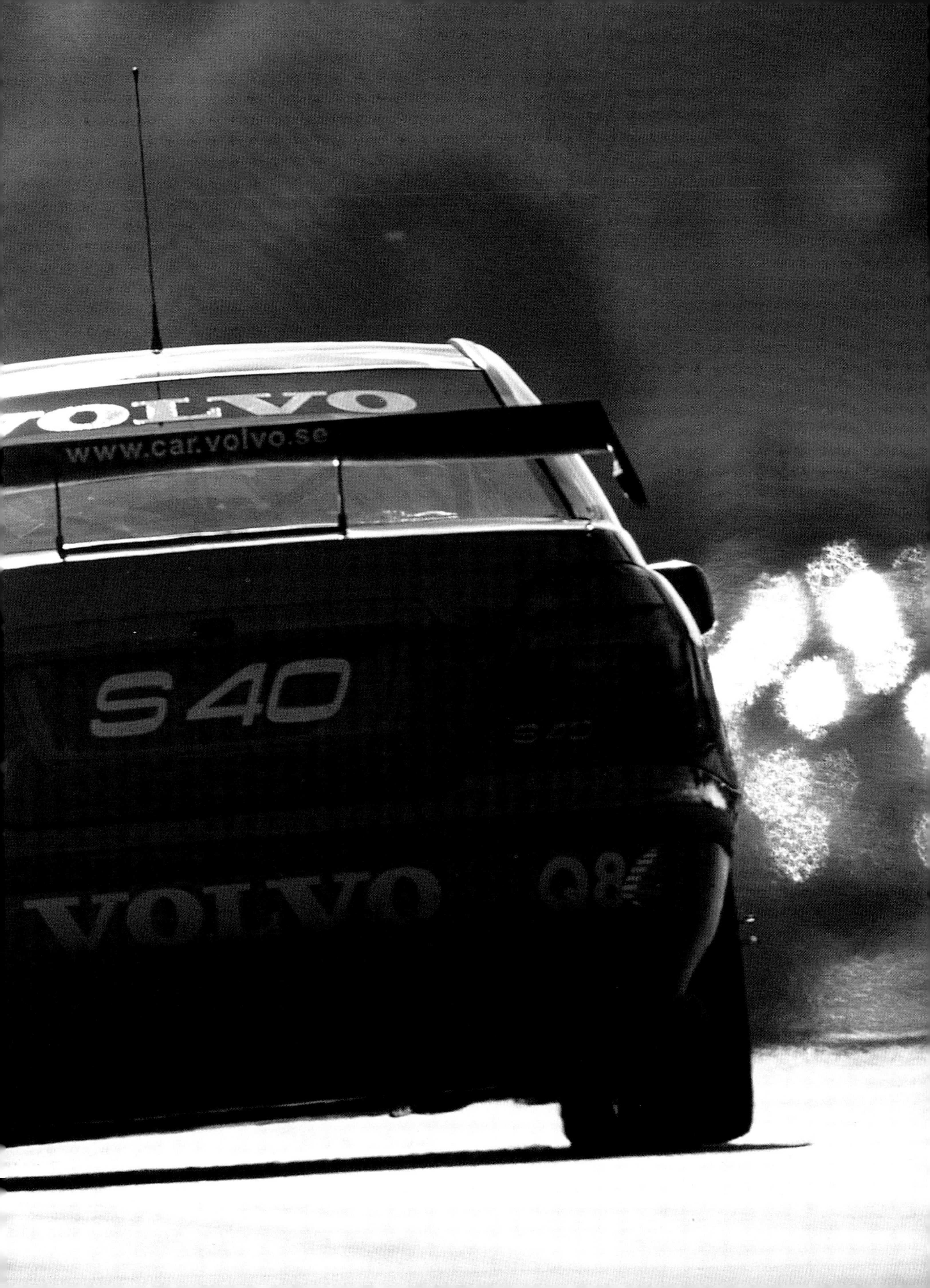
VOLVO
www.car.volvo.se
S40
VOLVO
Q8

The most exciting battle

David Owen-Smith - Auto Trader

Auto Trader is delighted to congratulate Rickard Rydell on his success in winning the 1998 Auto Trader RAC British Touring Car Championship. We also extend our congratulations to Vodafone Nissan Racing and Nissan for their success in winning the teams' and manufacturers' trophies. The fact that nine different drivers and five teams won races is an indication of the superb racing that has been enjoyed throughout the 1998 season. The new race format including one-shot qualifying for the sprint race and pit stops in the feature race definitely worked, producing probably the most exciting title battle since 1992.

The determination of both drivers and teams ensured that once again both the public who braved the British weather and the armchair enthusiasts saw racing of the highest calibre fought out with the traditional and inevitable action.

Auto Trader would like to thank all those involved in the 1998 championship and especially those behind the scenes who made the event possible. But most of all we extend our thanks to the spectators and fans for continuing to support the world's best touring car series.

The 1999 Auto Trader Touring Car Championship starts in April at Donington Park. Don't miss it!

LAT/JEFF BLOXHAM

A talent showcase

Peter Foubister – Publishing Director, AUTOSPORT

AUTOSPORT is privileged to have been able to sponsor the 1998 Independents' Cup. It is an important part of the Auto Trader British Touring Car Championship and an arena in which top-class teams and drivers can show off their talents in direct competition with the ultra-professional factory programmes. As such it represents a way for competitors to stretch and test themselves in the best traditions of the sport. Our congratulations go to Tommy Rustad for winning the Cup and to all the other competitors for their excellent efforts, particularly those giant-killing drives which threatened to win the £100,000 Alan Gow put up for the first independent overall winner. On our part, we have backed our sponsorship with better coverage than ever of the Independents' efforts in AUTOSPORT magazine and made it an integral part of our web site. Many of the AUTOSPORT Cup cars carried *www.autosportmag.com* stickers and visitors to the site have been able to access live BTCC timing screens. A link-up with Motor Sports Timing allows us to show all the qualifying and race times from both the BTCC and support races on the TOCA bill. In 1999 we will be improving and expanding the information we post on the website and look forward to welcoming old friends and new friends both there and at the circuits.

BRYN WILLIAMS

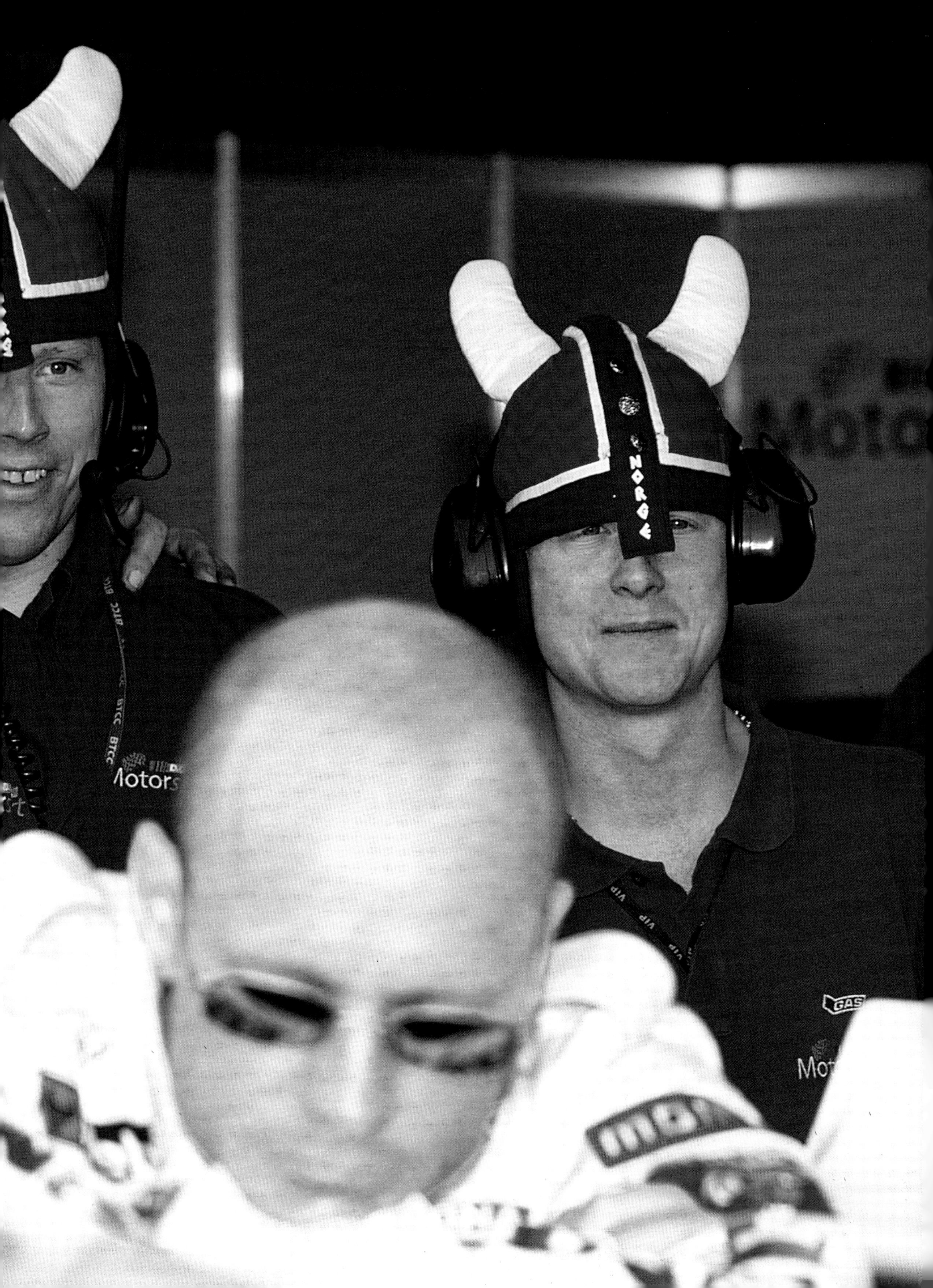
NORGE
BTCC

THE SAN FRANCISCO

POLICE DEPARTMENT

SAY YOU CAN ONLY

GO DOWN THIS HILL.

VOLVO BEG TO DIFFER.

Two things made this demonstration possible. The permission of the SFPD, and the class-leading torque of the 200bhp turbocharged Volvo S40 T4
The Volvo S40. From £13,995. For more details call 0800 11 40 40. www.volvo.com Car featured Volvo S40 T4 with metallic paint £20,955.

VOLVO

THE VOLVO S40 T4
A CAR YOU CAN BELIEVE IN

A big noise on the quiet

Family man, Swedish national hero and now British Touring Car Champion, life for Rickard Rydell is sweet at the moment. This shy man has found his 1998 season with Volvo deeply satisfying. Jon Noble tells his story

LAURENCE BAKER

Rickard Rydell acknowledged his British Touring Car Championship title with not a bang but a whimper. As a seething mob of his loyal Swedish fans chanted their joy at the success of their country's latest sporting hero, exactly 20 years after they had lost Ronnie Peterson and Gunnar Nilsson, the man himself could merely smile.

But that says everything about Rydell. He is a quiet family man who would never become involved in the kind of amateur dramatics all too often displayed by some of his rivals. Rydell is the epitome of the perfect, polished, ultra-professional role model that Volvo clearly love having on their books.

On top of all that, he is also a very quick racing driver. A former Swedish kart champion, he cut his teeth in Formula 3 single seaters in Sweden and then Britain under the guidance of mentor Picko Troberg, a major figure in the Swedish motorsport world. He later switched to Japan, where he diced with Jacques Villeneuve and Anthony Reid for the 1992 Formula 3 title.

His career in the Far East had seemed to reach something of a plateau by the end of 1993 before Volvo, embarking on a BTCC campaign, opted to sign him up. The first year was acknowledged to be a bit of a 'fun' marketing exercise with the 850 estate by Tom Walkinshaw, boss of TWR Racing which has run the Volvo touring car programme from day one. It

Above: Rickard's singing Swedish fans were out in force at Silverstone to serenade their new national hero

did not bring success – but that did not take long to follow and Volvo won races in its second BTCC season.

Since 1995 he has regularly challenged at the front for victories; finished third in the championship twice, and this season he capped it all with the BTCC drivers' title and victory in the end-of-season Bathurst 1000 kilometres race.

And although few would believe it from the outside, inwardly Rydell is still over the moon about what he describes as his 'best season ever' in motor racing, which netted him his first racing car championship.

'I've had several good years in the sport and won plenty of races, but this season has been better than any previously,' he says. 'It has been a big achievement for me and the team, but I don't think the people in Britain understand just how important this win is for Sweden and Volvo.

'About 10 per cent of the Swedish population watch the BTCC on television. They are amazing viewing figures, and I think from next year there will be more and more people watching.

'There were at least 50 people at that final race from the Anderstorp Motor

LEFT: BOTHWELL PHOTOGRAPHIC. FAR LEFT: LAT/PETER J FOX

Left: Rickard's mentor Picko Troberg joined the crowd on his victory day. Below left: Rydell's BTCC machines – an 850 estate, the saloon version and the S40

BOTHWELL PHOTOGRAPHIC

Club, who have been supporting me throughout my career, and there were also a lot of Swedes at the penultimate race, which was nice. This championship is not just a national one, it has a huge international following.'

Rydell is exactly the kind of sporting hero Sweden has been looking for since the deaths of Peterson and Nilsson during that awful 1978 season and the retirement of tennis superstar Bjorn Borg in the early Eighties.

'That was when Swedish motorsport died,' says Rydell of that 1978 season. 'People stopped writing about it and even in the Eighties there was not that much coverage. When Volvo entered the BTCC a few bits were written and then suddenly the television interest took off.

'Now it is unbelievable. There are articles all the time, not just on the BTCC, but also on Formula 1, and motor racing features a lot more than some other sports.

'There are about three times as many viewers for the BTCC as there are for F1, which wasn't even on terrestrial television last season. It's getting bigger and better and I think even the success of Mika Hakkinen, a Scandinavian, in F1 has played its part.'

The BTCC's position in the Swedish entertainment industry is like that of EastEnders here, broadcast on weekday evenings with a massive following, and Rydell is a household name. He features on the front covers of magazines and newspapers and is a regular on television.

'He is as popular as Bjorn Borg ever was,' revealed Johan Thoren, Swedish television sports presenter. 'He has got a massive following, as big as for a film star or musician, and his popularity is made even greater because he is shy and keeps himself to himself.'

It is clear to everyone that Rydell has not let the success of it all go to his head. He may well take his job more seriously

these days, having used a personal trainer for the past two seasons, and he may be the first to admit that he is a 'quiet' man, but that is not to say he did not enjoy winning the BTCC crown.

'I was really happy at the time, but until I had crossed the finish-line at Silverstone I had not really thought about winning the championship,' he continues. 'I knew I had the chance of the title beforehand, but I just wanted to make sure I did my job as well as I could. It was important to make no mistakes.

'And only when I crossed the line did I start thinking about the title and everything it meant. It was hard to take everything in and even now, a few weeks afterwards, I am still really happy that I did it. I mean it: I am really happy.'

Rydell's public image is no different from that which the team sees. He is not the kind of man to smile and share a joke with the mechanics one minute and then throw his dummy out of the pram the next. He maintains an even keel throughout – politely thanking individual team members for their efforts and working calmly through the troubles as well as the success.

'I'm still quiet and relaxed when I am with the team,' he says. 'I don't often show emotions and don't think it is so important to either.' But there was one moment when Rydell did let his emotions get the better of him. At Brands Hatch in late-August, as the title fight with Anthony Reid raged on, he grabbed his rival by the throat to voice his anger at an on-track move from the Nissan driver.

It was an action that surprised many and, according to Reid, was so out of character that many felt Reid must have done something serious. Sure enough, Reid had the victory taken away from him.

Rydell, however, sees the incident as nothing out of the ordinary and is keen to forget all about it. 'I didn't think it was the

LAT/PETER J FOX

LAT/MALCOLM GRIFFITHS

Top: Rydell in full flow in the S40 which helped him to glory. Above: A moment of contemplation for one of the BTCC's quieter characters

big deal that everyone was making it out to be,' he claims. 'I've seen at least ten similar incidents between drivers, but it was only because mine was on television that everyone took notice.

'A similar thing happened at the same race when Nigel Mansell went up to Tiff Needell, but I never heard anything about that. The fact that this happened in the public eye made it ten times worse, but that is just media over-reaction. There is no animosity between Anthony and I.'

In fact, you could hardly imagine animosity building up between Rydell and anyone else. Like title-winning predecessor Alain Menu, the Swede has a life which revolves round his family. His wife Ulrika was reduced to tears when he clinched the championship at Silverstone, although his children, Emma, Lisa and Max, were perhaps a little too young to fully realise the importance of the occasion.

'The family are the most important thing to have around if you want to have a happy life. When you have a family, racing has to come second. But at the same time, both things are very important and they have got to go together.

'You can't have a happy life if you do not have a good family, and you cannot be successful as a racing driver if you do not have a happy life away from the race tracks. This year, I have been very happy on all counts.'

While some people like to say that racing drivers become one second a lap

slower for every child they have, Rydell seems to be getting quicker and quicker. TWR Team boss Tom Walkinshaw certainly has no complaints.

'Rickard's professionalism and application are among the best,' he says. 'He is very, very quick and he is focused on the job he has to do. He's done a superb job for several years now and we might even give him a little treat for winning the championship… in one of our black (TWR Arrows F1) cars.

'It is clear he is one of the best drivers in touring car racing. We've watched him grow with us, we complement each other: we get the best out of him and he gets the best out of us. The combination is the best that is around at the moment.'

Life does seem to be moving fast for Rydell. The BTCC crown, victory in Bathurst and the promise of an F1 test. As the BTCC's appeal continues to rise, Rydell has less and less time to himself.

That means less time spent with his family, less time working for the family flower business and less time spent on the family's boat in the summer.

But it also means more happiness, more satisfaction and more popularity. 'At the moment I'm really enjoying life,' he smiles. 'As long as the BTCC remains as big as it is now, then I am happy to stay there.

'Of course I would love to be racing for a top team in F1 but it is not realistic to expect that to happen. I'm happy with all that I have got at the moment…'

Prime Sponsor RAC British Touring Car Championship

1 9 9 3
1 9 9 4
1 9 9 5
1 9 9 6
1 9 9 7
1 9 9 8

Way out in front

Auto Trader is proud to be in its sixth great year as prime sponsor of the RAC British Touring Car Championship.

We would like to extend to all this year's entrants and our millions of readers best wishes for their personal success and safe motoring throughout the year.

Auto Trader 98 BTCC

No.1 in buying and selling cars

Off the factory line

Running a BTCC programme is a major operation. Ray Mallock Ltd's huge factory looks more like a Nissan production line.
Photos: LAT/Martyn Elford

Top left: RML devotes 20,000 square feet of its factory exclusively to the Nissan project. Above: Stocks are impressive - all the wiring to keep three electricians busy full time; 200 different specs of damper; 200 wheels for three cars; and enough front bumpers - the team damages six a weekend on average. Left: A complete stickered-up set of bodywork is always ready for each car. Far left. All welding and fabrication can be carried out in-house

Left: There are 80 pipes
on each car and spares
are kept for all of them.
Above: Trophies are the
reward. **Above right:**
The sub-assembly
department looks after
gearboxes and uprights

Left: Vodafone Nissan Racing has three trucks – two artics and a 17-ton support vehicle. The artics are both self-sufficient. Everything needed to run the race cars is on-board. Below: The focus of all the human and technical resources – the Nissan Primera GT which won two 1998 BTCC titles

At RML's factory in Wellingborough, 40 staff worked full time to ensure the Primera GT became and remained the best car in the BTCC

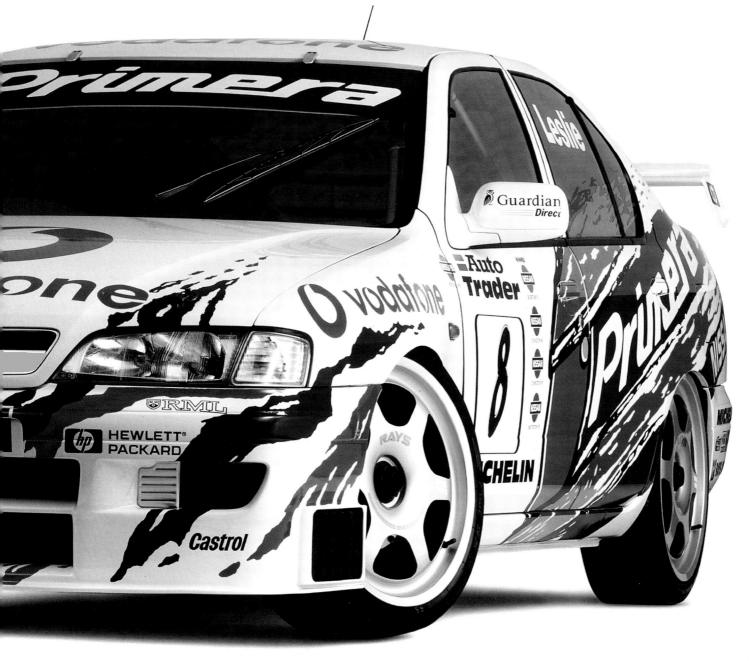

COURTESY OF TBWA GGT SIMONS PALMER LIMITED

Who is the BTCC's best?

Charlie Cox is one of the BTCC lads. He used to race, now he commentates. He is perfectly placed to judge this year's top touring car performers

CHARLIE COX'S TOP 10 BRITISH TOURING CAR CHAMPIONSHIP DRIVERS

CHARLIE COX

Australian Cox has taken over from Murray Walker as the BBC's voice of the BTCC. A man with trenchant views on all manner of subjects, he knows a good tin-top pedaller when he sees one. And he also has the inside knowledge that came from a season contesting the BTCC, which included one of the series' biggest ever accidents

2 ANTHONY REID

The Nissan ace could so easily be top of this list. Although his championship hopes were wrecked by his poor start to the year, he proved to be a strong, predatory driver and his second half of the season was almost perfect. He took defeat like a man and will be a great credit to Ford.

3 JAMES THOMPSON

His second season at Honda proved that the Yorkshireman is getting better and better. He forced his Accord to win races and I would put his drive in the penultimate round of the series at Silverstone as the best of the year. It was a fiery performance and deserves credit.

1 RICKARD RYDELL

It just had to be Rydell at number one. That is not just because he won the championship but because he did not crumble when the pressure came and it mattered most. He gave us all a fright at Oulton Park, but when he had a job to do at Silverstone, he lifted himself to the challenge and came on strong.

4 YVAN MULLER

Simply spectacular. He brought to the BTCC the kind of driving skills that he had honed in ice racing. Through the Esses at Croft he gave me the most awe inspiring sight of the year. The Audi may not have been the best car but he drove every lap as a qualifying lap.

5 ALAIN MENU

Mr Cool has dropped down a couple of spots during his title defence by letting some midfield traffic ruffle his feathers. Just look at what happened in the finale at Silverstone when he got involved with John Cleland – on and off the track. But I still think he is a supreme driver.

6 JASON PLATO

Just behind Menu on the list, he was only just behind him on the track as well. His second season in touring cars may have only brought one victory, but I believe he was much improved and that there are greater things to come. Very good in traffic and working up through the field.

7 DAVID LESLIE

After a strong start to the year, becoming the first man to win two races in 1998, he was overshadowed by Nissan team mate Anthony Reid. He still proved he has blinding speed and if I had to put my money on somebody to bring the car home I would put it on Leslie.

8 JOHN CLELAND

With a better car in his hands, John proved that he can still do it and that he hasn't forgotten how to race. Plus he showed time and again this year that he has still got the reflexes to be one of the best starters in the business. Give him a glimpse of the lead and he's off like a rabbit.

9 WILL HOY

His second year at Ford was one of frustration but there were a couple of highlights on the way. He won the team's first race for three years in changeable conditions at Silverstone and showed well as occasional team mate to one of the world's greatest drivers.

10 MATT NEAL

Here because of his strong 1998 qualifying performances that landed him in the thick of the action with the works drivers. But his tangles with them in the races impaired his finishing rate.

The lion roars again

Nigel Mansell made his return to racing in the British Touring Car Championship this year. The fans loved him, but his rivals took a bit more convincing. Mark Skewis canvassed opinion

BOTHWELL PHOTOGRAPH

On board telemetry showed that Mansell carried more speed into the fast corners than Ford team-mate Will Hoy

He's back. And this time it's personal. Or at least Nigel Mansell *thought* it was personal when he returned to racing with a bang. Quite literally. No sooner had Ford enticed the former F1 and IndyCar champ out of retirement, than the BTCC field appeared intent on ramming him back into it.

The final four outings of his six-race campaign were marred by incidents, leading Mansell to complain: 'I felt as if I had a bullseye on the back of the car.'

Rivals insist his persecution complex is as big as his bank balance. But Dick Bennetts, whose West Surrey Racing outfit prepared Mansell's cars, suggests that it wasn't only the autograph hunters who targeted his driver.

'I think some of the guys picked on him.' he says. 'A few of them attracted themselves to red 55 as if it was a magnet, and I'm sure there was an element of "I'm not afraid to show him..." Either that, or one car had a hell of a lot of bad luck!'

John Cleland, the sport's elder statesman, thinks claims that Mansell was deliberately targeted are unfounded. 'This has been the most brutal season I can remember - and I can remember a few!' he concedes. 'But as for the idea of us beating Nigel up, no way. It's not as if we all got

together in the gang house and decided to teach the new kid a lesson. If we had, he wouldn't have got as far as he did.'

Not that he got far on the last occasion he raced in this country, five years ago. Then, Mansell's touring car debut made a big impact. Both on the fans and the bridge support into which he believes he was pushed. Upon signing for Ford, he declared the event had left 'unfinished business'. For whom you wondered, as early testing was punctuated by incidents.

One collision led Vauxhall's PR agency to issue a release entitled: 'Mansell finds new Vectra a big hit'. It was an ingenious attempt to generate publicity on the back of Ford's outlay on a superstar. It also established that Mansell was a big name up there to be shot down.

It was quickly evident that he had little chance of escape in the Mondeo: its engine lacked driveability; its chassis lacked grip in slow corners, and welcomed long bends as a vampire would sunrise.

When you sign Mansell, though, you sign melodrama. Just hours after thumping his car hard into the tyres in his comeback race, he produced one of his finest drives to star in what has been acclaimed as the best touring car scrap ever.

The script was better suited to TV's

Dallas than it was to Donington: from the torrential rain which transformed the Mondeo from beast into beauty, to the pace car which bunched the field, and his sensational rise from last to first, it was a fairy tale. He was eventually classified fifth but had already won respect, however begrudging, from rivals. 'I learned from following him that the guy is exceptionally brave,' explains eventual victor Cleland. 'Or stupid.'

It was a hard act to follow. Expectations had risen, but opponents' opinions of him slid in the opposite direction after a sequence of on- and off-track altercations. As the honeymoon ended, so the squabbling began.

For five years Mansell has blamed Tiff Needell for the accident which spectacularly ended his debut, and he could suppress his anger no longer when the pair renewed their rivalry with a clash at Brands Hatch. 'He came up to me and said, "I've forgiven you once, I'm not prepared to do it again," recalls Needell. 'He put his hand on my face and suggested I might like to clear off down the other end of the pit lane before we sorted things out properly. I laughed and asked him when he was going to apologise for spoiling *my* races.'

LAT

Above: Cleland claims that if the BTCC field had wanted to take Mansell out they would have done a better job

BOTHWELL PHOTOGRAPH

Above: TOCA boss Alan Gow dismissed claims that Mansell was targeted

BOTHWELL PHOTOGRAPHIC

Above: Red Five returns. Below: The famous eyes of the People's Champion

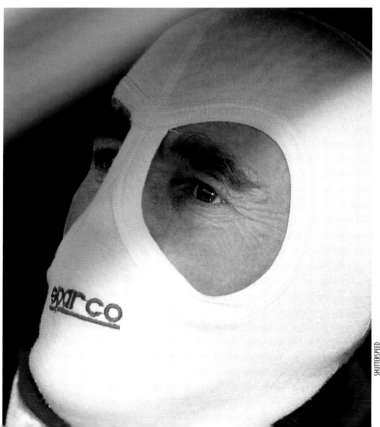

SHUTTERSPEED

AUTOSPORT Cup privateer Mark Lemmer also traded paint with Mansell. And words. 'He's paranoid,' says Lemmer. 'Sure, a few jokes went around the paddock, but why would we mess up our own races to spoil his? I'm sure he felt we should give him extra respect, but we were all fighting for the same bit of tarmac.'

Mansell's humour, like his car, took a battering at Brands, and his frustration boiled over when he was penalised for exceeding the pit lane speed limit by just four kph. 'They can get stuffed,' he responded over the car-to-pit radio. They didn't, but he was: the moment was recorded for posterity on *Grandstand*.

He refused television crews further access in the wake of that video nasty. His car was televised for just 23 seconds at the season finale...

Paranoia, or simply a marked man? One of his assailants, Derek Warwick, who punted his former F1 adversary out of the points at Silverstone, is an unlikely ally in the debate. 'There's a bit of the Old Boy syndrome in the BTCC,' he reveals. 'A lot of drivers feel very aggrieved by the pull, the money and the publicity that a former grand prix star can bring. When I came into the series I realised there was a feeling of: "Let's put this upstart in his place".

'For a while I think I had a target on the back of my car too. I'm not convinced that people deliberately looked for Nigel on the track, but I do think some of them jumped on the bandwagon after the races.'

Mansell believes the show would be even better if the hooligan element was removed. 'There were a whole host of incidents, not just with myself,' he stresses. 'In my opinion, 50 per cent of them could be totally avoided. That would make for even closer and better racing.'

Nor does he accept that the brutality has to come with the territory. Instead, he cites the example of Donington, where he engaged Warwick, Cleland and David Leslie in a colossal battle. 'We nudged, we leant, we pushed, and occasionally we hit, but without anyone falling off the circuit,' he says. 'It proves these cars can be driven hard and professionally without accidents.'

Did he expect the rough and tumble that greeted him? 'After Donington and Brands, I can honestly say I could expect anything,' comes the pointed reply.

If Mansell doesn't top many BTCC insiders' Christmas card list, that is not to suggest that his comeback was anything but a resounding success in many areas.

The series itself was the biggest winner, for it was exposed to a wider audience and found greater credibility with its existing one. 'A few years ago the BTCC was regarded as God's waiting room for drivers, a place where they could cruise round and collect money for the retirement fund,' acknowledges Gow. 'We've moved away from that now, and anyone could see that Nigel wasn't just playing.'

You suspect he would gladly set aside two more seats in the "waiting room" if, as seems likely, former champs Jody Scheckter and Alan Jones follow in Mansell's footsteps.

The project left a dent in Ford GB's budget, as well as its car, for it is reputed to have lavished half a million pounds to lure its man out of retirement. The move

hit opposition higher up the parent company, where it was suggested his presence could be a PR time bomb waiting to explode. At times, you could almost hear the ticking.

Ultimately, the only explosion was in television coverage. Audits revealed that his Donington heroics benefited Ford branding to the tune of £1.3 million - up from £200,000 at a typical race. In one hit, the manufacturer had recouped its investment three-fold.

In truth, Mansell did more for Ford than it did for him. Having gone to such lengths to capture a high-profile name, the company scored an own goal by curtailing the Mondeo's development after a mid-season decision to switch teams for '99.

'The initial approach was to test and help develop the car, culminating in three races. I was told that the resources would be there to move the team forward very quickly,' reveals Mansell. 'Part of my motivation was to help a team we all knew was not competitive make progress. In the early stages that seemed to be the case, and it was very rewarding. Then the goalposts moved for us all halfway through the year.'

If his comeback wasn't a success in terms of results, it was still a reminder of pure racing ability. 'It's a bit like asking Linford Christie to give up sprinting and run a marathon as quickly as the long-distance experts,' explains Warwick, who has seen the front-wheel drive formula ruin many a good reputation. 'No amount of talent can compensate for the experience the top guys here have.'

Ford team mate Will Hoy marvels not only at Mansell's on-track bravery, but his courage at embarking upon the programme at all. 'It took a lot of guts for somebody with his record to put his head on the block,' he says. 'Very few drivers would do that. He knew it would be easy to end up with egg on his face.'

'For half a million quid, I'd put my reputation on the line,' argues one rival, but Mansell's motivation was never financial. He genuinely believed that with the right support the Mondeo could run at the front, if not win races. Ford's strategic withdrawal left him high and dry. If he returns again, it will be with a manufacturer he feels is prepared to look after his image, as well as its own.

He at least drew some solace from the rise in BTCC attendances which reflected the 44-year-old's enduring appeal to spectators. While they voted with their feet, the circuits had to show their support with something more substantial. Their contributions to Mansell's purse were nevertheless rewarded with an estimated 5,000 rise in attendance.

'He has a great affinity with the man in the street,' explains Donington Park spokesman Dave Fern. 'I've seen him spot a disabled kid in the middle of a crowd, and insist that he was brought into the pit garage for the afternoon. His fans see a different side to the man.'

His comeback demonstrated that what you see is what you get with Nigel Mansell. He's still fast, committed, and, let's be honest, a sore loser. But if he never wins another race, the indications are that he will always be 'The People's Champion'.

Spice up your life

TOCA gambled on a series of rule changes for 1998 in a bid to make the show more exciting. Charles Bradley analyses their success

FAR LEFT: BOTHWELL PHOTOGRAPHIC. LEFT: PETER J FOX. RIGHT/LAT/JEFF BLOXHAM

This was the year in which TOCA rounded off some of the rough edges of the Auto Trader British Touring Car Championship and introduced new qualifying and race formats in a bid to spice up the action.

Add to that an easing of the driving standards regulations, which allowed even more contact than usual, and you had a recipe for one heck of a year's racing.

The opening qualifying session remained the same as ever - a half hour free-for-all of looking for a clear lap - which decided the feature race grid. But the real acid test was the One-Shot Showdown which settled the grid for the shorter Sprint Race, where the drivers had but one chance to set a time.

The format proved a success straight away. And, surprisingly, it was Mr. One-lap Wonder himself, '97 champion Alain Menu, who blew it at the season opener by straight-lining the chicane and having his times disallowed. Then, two weeks later, he spun off at Silverstone and had to start at the back again. 'If it was TOCA's aim to shake up the grid then it's worked, hasn't it?' he rued. Yup.

But it was the double-length Feature Race which really added the element of uncertainty. Mandatory pit stops were a novelty at the start of the year but soon became a crucial tactical minefield.

The issues were many. Stop early and your tyres would be shot at the end of race. Pit late and you would lose out to those who had stopped early during the middle stages.

Then there was the problem of rejoining in traffic, plus congestion in the pit lane itself. And which tyres to change? Both fronts or the left-hand side? The latter gave the optimum grip on the all-important out lap. Choices, choices.

'It's great because it gets the team involved in a completely different way,' said new champion Rickard Rydell. His Volvo team boss, Tom Walkinshaw, agreed: 'It's added another dimension to it. Teams can now have an influence in winning and losing a race.'

Pit lane safety was a pre-season concern but, despite a few near misses, the only collision was between Menu and Yvan Muller at the Thruxton pit lane exit. Luckily there were no serious consequences from that incident.

Some teams took advantage of the stops, while others took quite a while to get their act in order. Others raced for the point on offer to anyone who led the Feature Race. That turned the Oulton Park race in May upside-down when Paul Radisich - striving to score a point in the tardy Peugeot - crossed the path of 'real leader' Menu, which ultimately led to the

Renault star losing what looked like a certain victory.

But the inclusion of the changes met with almost universal acclaim: 'You have to say that TOCA made the right choice,' said Audi's motorsport manager, Dr Wolfgang Ullrich. 'Things such as this have pluses and minuses, so you have to try them or you will never know if they'll be successful or not. I think it's helped it to be a thrilling championship right until the end.'

Another change which helped 1998 to be a year of fine vintage was the new driving standards code. In essence, the BTCC became a contact sport with one proviso: knock someone off the track and you'll be endorsed and fined. But there was a good deal more freedom to tap and lean than there had been in the past.

Some people didn't like it; some didn't get the gist of the idea until they'd been given a 'serve' from behind. Lesson one in the new-look BTCC: hit first, answer questions later in the TOCA sin bin.

Cast your mind back to Donington in May and the bruising battle between Rydell and Anthony Reid and you'll see a motorsport duel of the highest entertainment value. Again and again, Rydell slammed into the back of the Nissan at the chicane in an attempt to unsettle it enough to dive through.

Far left: Pit-stops became a regular feature. Above left: The role of the team was more important than ever. Above right: Pit-stop kings Williams

But Reid stayed resolute and held his place, proving that the new laws didn't play into the hands of the aggressor completely. They merely gave him a licence to thrill.

Changes to the prize fund meant that if a driver won every race then he'd go home with a cool million pounds. While that scenario was highly improbable, more likely to go was the £100,000 on offer to any Independent Cup runner who won a race outright.

This was the year when TOCA innovated and experimented like never before. Next season there's a night race at Snetterton and the use of the Island circuit layout at Oulton Park

It's a case of offering the public something new when, after all, it's actually the tried and tested formula that keeps thousands of them on the edge of their seats all year.

Running after Rickard

The rest of the BTCC field was left to play catch up as Rickard
Rydell drew clear in the title chase after some early challenges.
Marcus Simmons tells the story of how the Swede came out top

LEFT: PETER J FOX. PREVIOUS PAGE: LAT/GAVIN LAWRENCE.

Just as Alain Menu did in 1997, Rickard Rydell this year finally laid to rest his ghost of never having won a championship title. The Swede fully deserved his success in the Auto Trader British Touring Car Championship.

Rydell, who celebrated his 31st birthday two days after clinching the drivers' title at the final meeting, had a nail-biting season. He sprinted out of the stalls with a TWR Racing-run Volvo S40 which virtually melted the Thruxton tarmac at the opening meeting, but found the going tougher as the season wore on.

Reigning champion Menu, in his fifth season with the Renault Laguna, was a major challenger. So was James Thompson, whose Honda Accord was fine in qualifying but struggled to cling onto the leaders during the races.

But it was Anthony Reid who emerged as Rydell's rival over the final meetings. The Scot, who had lived the life of a racing mercenary as he travelled around the world to earn his living, had a slow start to his second BTCC season with the Ray Mallock Limited-run Nissan Primera GT. Soon, however, he became the man to beat. By mid-season Reid had taken his maiden BTCC win, at Donington Park, and by the end of the year he'd racked up a splendid seven victories – two more than champion Rydell.

It was difficult, going into the final meeting at Silverstone, to predict who would take the title. Reid was a good bet to win both races and if that happened, Rydell would need to finish both times on the podium.

In the end, TWR extracted the last ounce of speed out of the Volvo, and Rydell was able to win the title in style by finishing second in the penultimate round, three places ahead of Reid.

Rydell, who had spent the previous four seasons quietly becoming one of the best drivers in the BTCC, was supreme this season. The Volvo, which scrabbled for grip in slow corners, wasn't as good as the Nissan, and there were few occasions when Rydell could lead from the front.

This year, however, he was much better in the heat of battle – his defeat at Croft of David Leslie, Reid's Nissan team mate, was aggressive, spectacular and effective. Later in the season he knew exactly where to back off if need be; to concede places to drivers if he thought they might barge him off the track to get by. After a long apprenticeship in the BTCC's top four, Rydell had finally arrived.

Reid's year was a good deal more high-profile but less consistent. The title was lost to him in April, when Nissan gave Leslie the best of the equipment at the start of the season. Once a series of retirements had interrupted the older Scot's two early-season wins, there was little left to go for other than the manufacturers' championship. Nissan duly wrapped that up in the penultimate meeting at Oulton Park, but must have rued its lack of a clear focus at the start of the season.

Thompson made the best of a difficult final season for the Prodrive Honda team to nick third in the points from Menu at the last meeting. This was a great season from the 24-year-old Yorkshireman, who topped most of the winter test sessions but found the Honda difficult to drive because of its low-downforce aerodynamics.

Virtually every race ended with the pig farmer's son sweating like an, er, pig, but by mid-season Prodrive had worked successfully on getting a more consistent race set-up. Four wins followed for Thompson, who is gaining more and more respect from his initially patronising tin-top peers and should flourish and become a great champion.

A great champion already, Menu had an odd season in which he could be either brilliant or bruising. The Williams Renault won three times, twice after inspired drives at Thruxton, but crashed more frequently than any of the other major front runners.

Still the Swiss stayed in the title chase, even through a summer sequence of three heavy shunts, none of which were his fault. But the Laguna wasn't quite the force it was in 1997, and sometimes lacked

LEFT: PETER J FOX.

Top: The Peugeots spent much of the year chasing independent runners like Tommy Rustad. Above: The new pit stops brought pit lane fashion victims with them

LAT/PETER J FOX

LEFT: LAT/JEFF BLOXHAM. BELOW: BOTHWELL PHOTOGRAPHIC. BOTTOM BRYN WILLIAMS

Left: Menu was as quick as ever, but unable to re-live his 1997 days of glory. Top: Auto Trader's grid girls provided glamour. Middle: James Thompson extracted every last bit of speed from the Honda Accord. Above: Audi's John Bintcliffe battered a few panels...

LEFT: LAT/JEFF BLOXHAM

Above: Independent Matt Neal was a star. Right: The family appeal of the series was as strong as ever

grip compared to the awesome Nissan.

After bursting onto the scene in '97, this was always going to be a tougher season for Menu's team mate Jason Plato. He too stayed well in the hunt for honours for a long time, and seemed to be irritated when asked to play number two to Menu at Knockhill, for the pairing were still close in the points. Nevertheless, it was a good year for the Englishman, despite just one win, at Oulton Park.

Reid's team mate Leslie fell off the pace mid-season, seeming to bear the brunt of any Nissan engine problems going. He bounced back to lead the final round, and it was a disappointment that he failed to build on those two early victories.

Joining Leslie among the golden oldie comeback heroes this season were John Cleland, Derek Warwick and Will Hoy. This was a renaissance year for Cleland, or at least the first half of it was. Two wins at Donington Park lifted the Vauxhall veteran right to the forefront again. But, as the season progressed, the Triple Eight Vectra team fell from the pace, Cleland in particular was unable to get heat into his

tyres and so sometimes struggled for pace.

The 46-year-old Scot felt that the comparatively youthful Warwick, 44, was able to brutalise his tyres into submission with his more aggressive driving style. But, ironically, it was in tippy-toe soaking conditions that Warwick benefited from an inspired pit call at Knockhill to win his first race since his 1992 World Sportscar Championship season.

Cleland had the nastiest accident of the season, when he was unavoidably T-boned by Menu at Snetterton. He missed one meeting with rib injuries and on his return at Knockhill he introduced acupuncture to the BTCC, via needles in his ears.

Hoy too had a tactical success, when Ford works team West Surrey Racing made the weather call just right and got the V6 Mondeo into and out of the pits in double-quick time at Silverstone.

This was another character-building season for WSR, which was unceremoniously dropped by Ford in July in favour of Prodrive. And, while the Blue Oval went about signing up Menu and Reid for 1999, its '98 team was pretty

Clockwise from above right: Accidents (this one at Knockhill) stopped Cleland's momentum. Easy access to drivers was again a winning BTCC feature. Peugeots were rarely in any position to challenge Renaults. Ford was mostly stuck in the mud again.

much ignored for the rest of the year.

Former World Champion Nigel Mansell discovered just what an uncompetitive proposition the Mondeo was on his outings at Brands Hatch and Silverstone, but at least he was able to shine in the wet in a memorable outing at Donington Park.

Despite not winning a round, Frenchman Yvan Muller was a star of the series. With four-wheel drive now illegal for factory cars in Super Touring, Audi was forced to switch to the front-drive A4, which had been developed by triple ice-racing champion Muller around a very low-downforce aero kit.

With his sensational car control, Muller wowed audiences up and down the country with a string of stunning performances, and was promptly signed up by Vauxhall for 1999.

Muller was the BTCC newcomer who did well. Others, like Honda's Peter Kox, Volvo's Gianni Morbidelli and Ford's Craig Baird, had difficult seasons, as did third-year Audi man John Bintcliffe and Peugeot's veteran driver pairing of Paul Radisich and Tim Harvey.

Many of these guys frequently found themselves in the wheel tracks of independent competitor Matt Neal and his 1997-spec Team Dynamics Nissan. Neal was the fastest in the AUTOSPORT Cup for non-works drivers, but lost out to Norwegian Tommy Rustad, who took the title in his DC Cook Motorsport Renault Laguna, and Brookes Motorsport Honda Accord driver Robb Gravett.

All these drivers had their chance of glory, thanks to a series of measures introduced by BTCC organiser TOCA to even up competition and provide entertainment.

Most importantly for the independents, they were given tyre equality with the works teams by measures introduced over the winter to prevent favouritism. Michelin, with its near monopoly, understandably went more conservative on its supply than in 1997 – lap times might have been a tad slower as a result, but all were happy to be on the same rubber. Save perhaps Williams, which was said to have developed its car around the super-effective '101' tyre of '97.

For the crowds, the biggest changes were in race format. The first race at each meeting was shortened, and dubbed the sprint race, with the second – feature race – lengthened and including a compulsory pit stop to change two wheels. This was another area where the Nissans lost out initially, but later in the year Mallock's boys were beginning to make up ground on early-season pit pacesetters Williams, TWR and Prodrive. Qualifying procedure was changed too, with sprint race grids decided by a new, one-at-a-time Indy-style One-shot Showdown.

Tweaks like these helped keep the BTCC in the public eye. They might not go down well with the purists but, with manufacturer interest set to take a small dip, the series needs everything it can find to keep it attractive. Night racing, at Snetterton in July, will be 1999's major innovation.

Thanks in part to the changes already made, 1998 – an unpredictable, wild and sometimes thrilling year – was the best BTCC season for a long time. Especially if you were Swedish and drove a Volvo S40.

35

Rydell and Menu open the scoring

Rickard Rydell and Volvo may have dominated qualifying and the sprint race, but reigning champion Alain Menu fought back with a brilliant win for Renault in the new-format feature race

Truck Trader

Mobil 1
LAPS TO GO 32

Clockwise from right: Rydell and the Volvo were on form and stormed to an early points lead. The pack chases poleman Rydell at the start of the feature race. At the end of the feature it began to hail, but that didn't temper the Williams crew's joy at Menu's win. The first round of compulsory pit stops in the BTCC, livened up the race and worked a treat. The pit lane walkabout was as popular as ever

BOTHWELL PHOTOGRAPHIC

As the RAC British Touring Car Championship circus pitched its big top at Thruxton for the opening rounds of 1998, the cast prepared for a season which, on paper, had looked as open as any for some time.

Pre-season testing indicated that James Thompson and the Prodrive Honda Accord would be the combination to beat, but at Thruxton they were unceremoniously bumped from their position as title favourites by the ultra-competitive Volvo S40 of Rickard Rydell.

The series's new race formats - incorporating the short, sharp, sprint with its One-Shot Showdown qualifying session and the lengthened feature with its mandatory pit stops - had their first run-outs with resounding success.

Rydell was over a second up on the pack in the first qualifying session (the

LEFT & PREVIOUS PAGE: PETER J FOX

LAT/JEFF BLOXHAM

LAT/JEFF BLOXHAM

conventional half-hour one, which set the grid for the feature) and the prospect of Alain Menu-style domination loomed. Rickard duly won the sprint comfortably, despite being jumped at the start by Thompson and Jason Plato. Menu's title defence began disastrously when he became the first victim of the new One-Shot qualifying session. He over-cooked it on the way into the Club chicane, straight-lined it and had his time disallowed.

Between races, when asked about Rydell, Williams-Renault designer and engineer Mark Ellis warned that 'we've flattered him so far'. And so it proved, with Menu scoring a superb win demonstrating that he had absolutely no intention of giving up his title without a fight. Having fought his way up from the back to finish fifth in the sprint, Menu converted third on the grid into a win in

the feature, passing Rydell twice on the way. 'It was one of my best races ever – if not the best,' said Menu afterwards.

It had been a dramatic race with several cars spewing out fuel or oil and many drivers suffering from seriously impaired vision as their screens smeared.

At the end of the day, the signs were that Rydell and the Volvo would be the strongest combination, but it was also clear that plenty of others would be in the running. Thruxton is a quirky circuit and not always an accurate guide to form, but with Rydell on top, Menu snapping at his heels and Thompson close to the pace, it was looking good. It had also been well noted that Anthony Reid had put a Nissan, only completed just before the weekend, on the front row for the feature.

Best of all, the new formats had done all that was hoped of them.

ROUND 1	16 LAPS	**ROUND 2**	32 LAPS
DRIVER	**CAR**	**DRIVER**	**CAR**
1 Rickard RYDELL	Volvo S40	Alain MENU	Renault Laguna
2 Jason PLATO	Renault Laguna	Rickard RYDELL	Volvo S40
3 James THOMPSON	Honda Accord	James THOMPSON	Honda Accord
4 John CLELAND	Vauxhall Vectra	Jason PLATO	Renault Laguna
5 Alain MENU	Renault Laguna	Derek WARWICK	Vauxhall Vectra
6 Gianni MORBIDELLI	Volvo S40	John CLELAND	Vauxhall Vectra
7 David LESLIE	Nissan Primera GT	Peter KOX	Honda Accord
8 Anthony REID	Nissan Primera GT	Paul RADISICH	Peugeot 406
9 Yvan MULLER	Audi A4	John BINTCLIFFE	Audi A4
10 Peter KOX	Honda Accord	Matt NEAL	Nissan Primera GT

Fastest lap Rickard RYDELL
AUTOSPORT CUP Mark LEMMER

Fastest lap Alain MENU
AUTOSPORT CUP Matt NEAL

Hoy blooms in the spring rain

Will Hoy and West Surrey Racing did everything right to take an opportunist win in the wet feature race after David Leslie confirmed the Nissan Primera's pace with an easy sprint victory

THE ULTIMATE INDEPENDENT

The ultimate independent in the BTCC, Team Dynamics in partnership with Rimstock PLC, the U.K.'s premier independent manufacturer of light alloy wheels. Rimstock manufacture over 7,000 wheels per week for the 100+ and Team Dynamics ranges and are approved suppliers to the major car manufacturers.

For more information on 100+ and Team Dynamics Light Alloy Wheels,
Call: 0121 525 6500 Fax: 0121 525 8499 or visit our website @ www.rimstock.com

BOTHWELL PHOTOGRAPHIC. PREVIOUS PAGE: LAT/GAVIN LAWRENCE

If the pattern for the season looked to have been set at Thruxton, then all bets were off again after rounds three and four at Silverstone. Title favourites Rickard Rydell and Alain Menu had a disastrous weekend, managing just one fifth place (for Rydell) and three crashes between them, and the wins went to drivers who had had little joy at Thruxton.

The glory boys were David Leslie and Will Hoy. The Scot's win confirmed the suspicion that the Primera had become an even better car than it was at the end of 1997 (and that was pretty good). But Hoy's victory came out of the blue, aided by changing weather conditions and some great team work from West Surrey Racing.

Leslie's win was in the sprint and after he'd beaten poleman James Thompson's Honda Accord away from the grid, he dominated the race. Jason Plato was the Renault man on form this weekend and he took third place, pressurising birthday boy Thompson (now 24) towards the end.

Menu again fell foul of the One-Shot Showdown, spinning off at Becketts. Then his attempted charge up the field lasted less than a lap before he collided with AUTOSPORT Cup star Matt Neal.

The feature was a lot more complicated.

Plato led away, chased initially by Leslie and Menu, but at Abbey these two clashed. The rear suspension on Leslie's Primera broke in the impact, but he was unaware of this until he turned into Bridge and slewed into Menu's Laguna – end of story for both of them.

That left Plato ahead from Thompson and the gang. Until it rained and Plato lost the lead when he ran off the track at Becketts. They were already into the pit-stop window and now it was strictly a tactical race. The trick was to pit at the right time and change, quickly, to the right tyres. Plato's immediate stop for intermediates was not a bad call, but he'd lost a lot of time off the track. Thompson's stop a lap later was well-timed and quick, but the choice of wets was wrong.

The team that got it absolutely right was Ford. Hoy stayed out a couple of laps longer than Thompson, and when he stopped, WSR fitted a set of intermediate tyres in double-quick time. When it all settled down, Hoy was 20-seconds clear.

Plato and Reid (slow stop, but right tyres) scythed through the field, but Hoy was too far away and won by six seconds. Peugeot's Paul Radisich put in a strong run to fourth ahead of Gianni Morbidelli.

LAT/JEFF BLOXHAM

Top: David Leslie took Nissan's first BTCC win since 1993. **Above:** Plato leads away in the feature race. Leslie and Menu, behind, would not last the lap. **Left:** 'There were fishes out there this big.' Cleland Sr tells Cleland Jr about the conditions

BOTHWELL PHOTOGRAPHIC

ROUND 3	17 LAPS	**ROUND 4**	30 LAPS
DRIVER	**CAR**	**DRIVER**	**CAR**
1 David LESLIE	Nissan Primera GT	Will HOY	Ford Mondeo
2 James THOMPSON	Honda Accord	Jason PLATO	Renault Laguna
3 Jason PLATO	Renault Laguna	Anthony REID	Nissan Primera GT
4 Derek WARWICK	Vauxhall Vectra	Paul RADISICH	Peugeot 406
5 Rickard RYDELL	Volvo S40	Gianni MORBIDELLI	Volvo S40
6 John CLELAND	Vauxhall Vectra	Derek WARWICK	Vauxhall Vectra
7 Anthony REID	Nissan Primera GT	John CLELAND	Vauxhall Vectra
8 Gianni MORBIDELLI	Volvo S40	Yvan MULLER	Audi A4
9 Will HOY	Ford Mondeo	James THOMPSON	Honda Accord
10 Yvan MULLER	Audi A4	Craig BAIRD	Ford Mondeo

Fastest lap David LESLIE
AUTOSPORT CUP Robb GRAVETT

Fastest lap James THOMPSON
AUTOSPORT CUP Robb GRAVETT

Cleland back to his best

John Cleland took his first win since 1995, and Vauxhall's first since '96, in the sprint. That made it five different winners in the first five rounds. David Leslie then won the feature to become the first double winner of the year

45

LAT/MALCOLM GRIFFITHS

Above: Double joy for David Leslie and Nissan, the first to take a second win this year. Right: Peter Kox and the Honda head down the Craner Curves on the way to seventh in the sprint. Middle right: Cheer-up Thommo you've just moved into the points lead. Far right: Independent Matt Neal was a brilliant fifth

BOTHWELL PHOTOGRAPHIC

John Cleland made it five different winners from five rounds when he returned to the top step of the podium for the first time since 1995. Cleland's triumph came in the sprint, but then David Leslie immediately broke the pattern when he became the first double winner of the year in the feature.

Cleland's win came courtesy of a brilliant start from third on the grid. 'He started like a scalded cat,' admitted front row man James Thompson, who also beat pole-sitter Rickard Rydell into Redgate. Thompson could clearly run at least as

quickly as Cleland and closed right up, but he soon had to concentrate more on defending his place from Rydell, and the pressure on Cleland eased.

Ultimately the order remained the same as it had going into the first corner - Cleland, Thompson, Rydell - and the 1995 champion ended a win-less run that had lasted for far too long. 'The last couple of years have been terrible; I had almost forgotten what the podium was,' he admitted. It was also Triple Eight's first ever victory and Vauxhall's first win since Thompson lucked in at Snetterton in '96.

Once Jason Plato and Leslie had retired as a consequence of their squabble over fourth, Alain Menu took the place, ahead of AUTOSPORT Cup star Matt Neal, who was a competitive fifth overall in the Team Dynamics Nissan. No less than nine works cars trailed home in his wake.

In the feature, Leslie led away from pole and dominated the race. Menu held second initially, but a moment at Coppice let Cleland through to second. By the time he made his compulsory stop, Leslie had a healthy lead over Cleland. A relatively slow stop from the Triple Eight crew put the

PETER J FOX

BOTHWELL PHOTOGRAPHIC

Vauxhall well down, and back behind Menu, for whom Williams had done a typically slick stop, and Thompson.

By the end, Cleland had worked his way ahead of Thompson again to grab his second podium place of the weekend and set up the possibility of a serious title challenge. Plato put in a great drive to move up from the back of the grid to finish fifth, but that wasn't enough to preserve his brief championship lead. So another driver to have scored consistently but not yet win, moved to the top of the points table – Thompson.

ROUND 5		18 LAPS		ROUND 6		36 LAPS
	DRIVER	**CAR**			**DRIVER**	**CAR**
1	John CLELAND	Vauxhall Vectra		1	David LESLIE	Nissan Primera GT
2	James THOMPSON	Honda Accord		2	Alain MENU	Renault Laguna
3	Rickard RYDELL	Volvo S40		3	John CLELAND	Vauxhall Vectra
4	Alain MENU	Renault Laguna		4	James THOMPSON	Honda Accord
5	Matt NEAL	Nissan Primera GT		5	Jason PLATO	Renault Laguna
6	Yvan MULLER	Audi A4		6	Anthony REID	Nissan Primera GT
7	Peter KOX	Honda Accord		7	Rickard RYDELL	Volvo S40
8	Will HOY	Ford Mondeo		8	Derek WARWICK	Vauxhall Vectra
9	Tim HARVEY	Peugeot 406		9	Matt NEAL	Nissan Primera GT
10	John BINTCLIFFE	Audi A4		10	Yvan MULLER	Audi A4

Fastest lap David LESLIE
Autosport Cup Matt NEAL

Fastest lap David LESLIE
Autosport Cup Matt NEAL

Rydell racks up a maximum break

Two wins from pole position put Rickard Rydell and the Volvo S40 back into the points lead, and by a significant margin. Only Anthony Reid's Nissan offered any real opposition

Above: Rydell and Reid run side-by-side into Paddock. They were the class of the field but it was the Swede who had the edge. Right: Rydell, Reid and Menu spray the champagne on the sprint race podium

BOTH PICTURES: LAT/JEFF BLOXHAM

Rickard Rydell and the Volvo S40 took their only win of 1997 on the Brands Hatch Indy circuit. The Kent venue was where he really put the hammer down this season, winning rounds seven and eight and opening out the first significant points lead of the campaign.

Rydell began the weekend the way he intended to carry on, putting the S40 on pole for both races and, on a circuit where lap times are always very close but overtaking is tricky, he was in control throughout and went home with the season's only maximum score.

The man who challenged him hardest was Nissan's Anthony Reid, who at last looked able to translate the speed and promise he and the Primera had shown to date into a serious points-gathering run. He shadowed Rydell throughout the sprint and fought back from a time-consuming first lap clash with Honda's James Thompson, to finish third in the feature.

Alain Menu and the Renault weren't quite on the pace, but the Swiss still gathered a satisfying points-harvest with a third and fourth.

Fifth behind Menu in the feature was the astonishing Matt Neal in the AUTOSPORT Cup Nissan. Matt had the '98 aero kit on his car for the first time and he was flying. In the Sprint he'd been comfortably third behind Rydell and Reid, until he bent the front suspension when he attacked a kerb a little too hard. Then he'd also run third early in the feature, before

49

Clockwise from right: Rydell on pole. Matt Neal – a happy man. Mixing it with the best. Bintcliffe and Morbidelli in battle. Kox kicks up the gravel

dropping back behind Reid. He then lost more time at the pit stops to allow Menu up to fourth. Third on the grid for the sprint after the One-Shot Showdown and fifth fastest time in qualifying for the feature were perhaps even more impressive.

Prominent among the other top six men this weekend was Jason Plato, who was fourth in the sprint and unlucky to lose out on at least fifth in the feature, when his Laguna was hobbled by an electrical problem. He was joined in the first half dozen by John Cleland (sixth in the sprint), David Leslie (sixth in the feature) and Yvan Muller, who produced the best BTCC result to date for the front-drive Audi A4 with fifth place in the sprint.

Rydell's newly established series lead may only have been 15 points, or the reward for a sprint race win, but his tally of three wins and five poles to date was solid evidence of his form advantage at this early stage in the season.

LAT/PETER J FOX

BRYN WILLIAMS

ROUND 7		25 LAPS	ROUND 8		50 LAPS
	DRIVER	**CAR**		**DRIVER**	**CAR**
1	Rickard RYDELL	Volvo S40	1	Rickard RYDELL	Volvo S40
2	Anthony REID	Nissan Primera GT	2	James THOMPSON	Honda Accord
3	Alain MENU	Renault Laguna	3	Anthony REID	Nissan Primera GT
4	Jason PLATO	Renault Laguna	4	Alain MENU	Renault Laguna
5	Yvan MULLER	Audi A4	5	Matt NEAL	Nissan Primera GT
6	John CLELAND	Vauxhall Vectra	6	David LESLIE	Nissan Primera GT
7	Will HOY	Ford Mondeo	7	Peter KOX	Honda Accord
8	Paul RADISICH	Peugeot 406	8	John BINTCLIFFE	Audi A4
9	James THOMPSON	Honda Accord	9	John CLELAND	Vauxhall Vectra
10	John BINTCLIFFE	Audi A4	10	Gianni MORBIDELLI	Volvo S40

Fastest lap Anthony REID
Autosport Cup Tommy RUSTAD

Fastest lap Anthony REID
Autosport Cup Matt NEAL

Renault twins split the spoils

Alain Menu was shaping up for a double until he had a run-in with Peugeot's Paul Radisich. Jason Plato seized the moment and gave Renault its second victory of the day

PHOTOS: BOTHWELL PHOTOGRAPHIC AND (RIGHT) PETER J FOX

Anthony Reid leads Alain Menu and David Leslie into Fosters on the first lap of the feature. The Nissans lost out in the pits, Menu tangled with Paul Radisich and Jason Plato (right) won

LAT/MALCOLM GRIFFITHS

LAT/JEFF BLOXHAM

Top: Menu leads Plato and Rydell in the feature. Above: Warwick's damaged wheel from the sprint.

Oulton Park has become an established Alain Menu stomping ground in recent years and the Renault star was hoping to make real progress in his bid to retain the drivers' title. It all went to plan in the sprint, which yielded a win, but a bizarre two-part run-in with the struggling Peugeot 406 of Paul Radisich meant the second win went to his team mate Jason Plato.

Menu's win was as straightforward as any during 1998, with the Swiss ace leading from Rydell throughout. David Leslie was third in the Nissan and the only place-change in the top eight came courtesy of an uncharacteristic Honda engine blow-up for James Thompson.

Anthony Reid led the feature away from pole in his Nissan and looked well in control until it came to the pit stops. Then, both he and team mate Leslie, who had been third behind Menu, missed out badly, leaving Menu in control from Plato and Rydell.

That's when Radisich played his part. The New Zealander had stayed out as long as possible, bent on picking up a point for leading the race before he pitted. Menu caught him at Fosters and immediately dived for the inside line. Biffing the 406

out of the way, the Swiss driver delayed himself sufficiently to give Plato a run at him going into Knickerbrook.

Menu re-asserted his authority and resumed what looked like a winning drive, but five laps later the pesky Peugeot loomed up again. Radisich had pitted and then taken a stop-go penalty for speeding in the pit lane. He re-joined just ahead of the leaders. Menu came across him again at Fosters and made his move, but this time it went wrong for him. There was no contact, but the Laguna ran wide and Plato and Rydell were both by in a flash.

Menu was not a happy man, and his mood became even blacker when Reid demoted him to fourth place in a forceful move during which the Laguna's back bumper became detached. Thompson came home fifth, with Vauxhall's John Cleland sixth and, after the Honda driver's retirement in the sprint, the Scot became the only driver to have scored in every round to date.

Menu was clearly aware that an opportunity had been missed, while Rydell's pair of second places, on a track where both the Renaults and the Nissans had him beaten for pace, was a real bonus for his campaign.

LAT/JEFF BLOXHAM

LAT/MALCOLM GRIFFITHS

Above left: Rydell struggled for ultimate pace, but scored well. Left: Matt Neal's Nissan heads for the barriers at the start of the sprint

PETER J FOX

BOTHWELL PHOTOGRAPHIC

Above: Alain Menu kept up his winning ways at Oulton Park in the sprint. Right: Jason Plato celebrates his race win. Far right: Gianni Morbidelli was competitive at Oulton and finished sixth in the sprint

SHUTTERSPEED

ROUND 9	20 LAPS	**ROUND 10**	40 LAPS
DRIVER	**CAR**	**DRIVER**	**CAR**
1 Alain MENU	Renault Laguna	Jason PLATO	Renault Laguna
2 Rickard RYDELL	Volvo S40	Rickard RYDELL	Volvo S40
3 David LESLIE	Nissan Primera GT	Anthony REID	Nissan Primera GT
4 Jason PLATO	Renault Laguna	Alain MENU	Renault Laguna
5 Anthony REID	Nissan Primera GT	James THOMPSON	Honda Accord
6 Gianni MORBIDELLI	Volvo S40	John CLELAND	Vauxhall Vectra
7 John CLELAND	Vauxhall Vectra	Will HOY	Ford Mondeo
8 Will HOY	Ford Mondeo	John BINTCLIFFE	Audi A4
9 John BINTCLIFFE	Audi A4	Gianni MORBIDELLI	Volvo S40
10 Yvan MULLER	Audi A4	Yvan MULLER	Audi A4

Fastest lap Alain MENU	**Fastest lap** Anthony REID
AUTOSPORT CUP Tommy RUSTAD	**AUTOSPORT CUP** Tommy RUSTAD

//// D.C.COOK

We **win** on the track...

And we **won't** be beaten on any **deal off it**!!!

FOR THE BEST POSSIBLE DEAL AND
INSTANT QUOTATION TOGETHER
WITH THE **BEST SERVICE** ON ANY
NEW OR USED CAR, CALL
D.C.COOK FREE ON:

freephone **0800 7318092 NOW!**

**CREDIT,
PERSONAL
CONTRACT,
CONTRACT HIRE
AND LEASING
FACILITIES ARE
AVAILABLE**

Derby, Doncaster,
Manchester,
Morecambe,
Rochdale, York

Lincoln

Derby

Barnsley, Shrewsbury,
Wakefield

Barnsley, Derby, Doncaster,
Macclesfield, Manchester,
Morecambe, Rochdale,
Rotherham, Scunthorpe,
York

Aylesbury, St Albans

Doncaster

Derby

Blackburn, Bracknell,
Coventry, Derby, Leamington
Spa, Sheffield, Worksop

Crewe, Newcastle Under Lyme,
Northampton, Rotherham,
Slough

Derby, Morecambe,
South Shields

Barnsley,
Huddersfield, York

Lincoln

Bradford, Chesterfield,
Hull, Stoke, Wirral

IF YOU ARE INTERESTED IN MARKETING OR ENTERTAINMENT OPPORTUNITIES ASSOCIATED WITH

D.C.COOK MOTORSPORT PLEASE CONTACT **DAVID COOK** FOR INFORMATION ON: -

01709 373688 NOW OR FAX: 01709 820336

Join the **winning team**!

written quotations available subject to status   www.dccook.co.uk

Scots reign as racing hits heights

Anthony Reid set the pace and won a gripping sprint in fine style. But bad weather spiced up a feature race which included some of the best racing ever seen in the series, a starring role for Nigel Mansell, and victory for Vauxhall's evergreen John Cleland

LAT/PETER J FOX

Above: Thompson heads back into the feature race madness. Right: The Renault crew had little to cheer about. Above right: Nigel Mansell is as popular as ever. Far right: Mansell stirred the crowd's emotions on-track too, leading the feature race. Below right: Reid, Rydell and Hoy celebrate after the sprint

JOHN WILLIAMS

After a couple of meetings when overtaking was at a premium the BTCC really came alive at Donington with two of the best races the series has yet produced. There was overtaking galore, a maiden win for Anthony Reid, an unexpected second win of the season for John Cleland and a starring role for guest driver Nigel Mansell.

Reid broke his BTCC duck from pole in the sprint. 'It was a bit of a relief to be honest. I hope it's a turning point,' said the Scot after he'd endured early pressure from that man Cleland. JC had made a brilliant start to turn sixth on the grid into second at Redgate, but a safety car period after Mansell crashed heavily at Coppice, was his downfall. His rear tyres lost heat and he was unable to get them back up to

working temperature. That meant a drop to fifth by the end. Rickard Rydell took second place and Will Hoy a rather fortunate third. He had benefited both from Cleland's problems and the enthusiasm of Derek Warwick, who misjudged a move at Goddard and took out both Alain Menu and James Thompson.

Reid had looked well-set in the feature too until the weather played its part. With rain falling he had opted to swap to intermediates at the pit stops. Then the rain got harder and he spun out of the lead. That's when Cleland and Mansell swung into action.

Cleland had actually been running a strong third behind the fast-disappearing Nissans of Reid and David Leslie, until the rain got harder and he slid into and then

out of the gravel trap at Coppice. However the rain turned it all upside down again. Reid's demise came during a manic handful of laps, which saw as much overtaking as anyone could keep up with. 'It was just like dodgems out there,' admitted Leslie. Yvan Muller briefly took up the running, but then a biff knocked his wiper off the screen and he dropped back. Mansell took his turn in the lead, before being hunted down by Cleland and then Leslie and Warwick.

At the end it was veterans Cleland, Leslie and Warwick on the podium, with Mansell fourth on the road, but dumped to fifth behind Muller for overtaking under yellow flags. Matt Neal put in another excellent drive to finish sixth in the Team Dynamics Nissan.

LEFT AND PREVIOUS PAGE: LAT/PETER J FOX

LAT/GAVIN LAWRENCE

BOTHWELL PHOTOGRAPHIC

The BTCC's best?

Was this the best BTCC race ever? Its stars - and there were many of them - acclaimed it and for a few laps it took off and produced a level of action that should only be found in a cunningly edited TV sequence of the best moves of a whole season.

John Cleland was the winner and he was bubbled over with enthusiasm. 'It was an unbelievable race,' he said. 'I haven't got a clue what happened, I don't even know who was in the gaggle.'

That gaggle initially included Anthony Reid, David Leslie, John Cleland, Yvan Muller and Nigel Mansell. Reid, on unsuitable intermediate tyres soon spun out, but the others shuffled and re-shuffled positions constantly. 'It was a bit like dodgems, I got hit so many times, it was unreal,' admitted Leslie.

To add a further twist one of the race leaders was superstar guest Nigel Mansell who picked his way up through the pack when conditions were at their worst. Mansell has more than a little experience of exciting situations, but he too was impressed. 'It was fantastic,' he said, 'a great race and a clean race although I've never been hit so many times in my whole career.'

It was certainly exciting enough to vie for a place in any fan's memory as the best BTCC race ever. Its most obvious rival from recent years is the 1992 season finale at Silverstone. It buzzed with excitement throughout, not least in the battle between title hopeful Cleland and Steve Soper, team mate to eventual champion Tim Harvey. Soper dragged his battered BMW through the field to hunt down Cleland and try to demote him from a title-winning position. The result was a spectacular crash. That was a great, multi-layered race, but for sheer racing action Donington Park 1998 will take some beating.

ROUND 11	23 LAPS	**ROUND 12**	39 LAPS
DRIVER	**CAR**	**DRIVER**	**CAR**
1 Anthony REID	Nissan Primera GT	John CLELAND	Vauxhall Vectra
2 Rickard RYDELL	Volvo S40	David LESLIE	Nissan Primera GT
3 Will HOY	Ford Mondeo	Derek WARWICK	Vauxhall Vectra
4 Peter KOX	Honda Accord	Yvan MULLER	Audi A4
5 John CLELAND	Vauxhall Vectra	Nigel MANSELL	Ford Mondeo
6 Gianni MORBIDELLI	Volvo S40	Matt NEAL	Nissan Primera GT
7 Yvan MULLER	Audi A4	Gianni MORBIDELLI	Volvo S40
8 Robb GRAVETT	Honda Accord	Tommy RUSTAD	Renault Laguna
9 Jason PLATO	Renault Laguna	John BINTCLIFFE	Audi A4
10 Paul RADISICH	Peugeot 406	Roger MOEN	Honda Accord
Fastest lap Rickard RYDELL		**Fastest lap** Anthony REID	
AUTOSPORT CUP Robb GRAVETT		**AUTOSPORT CUP** Matt NEAL	

Above: Rickard Rydell was a winner again in the Volvo S40. Right: It was rough out there, with hard battles right down the field. Radisich, Neal and Hoy did their bit

LEFT: LAT/COLIN McMASTER ABOVE: PETER J FOX

Rydell grinds out another victory

It was fender-bending time at Croft and Rickard Rydell was in the thick of it as he produced one of his best wins of the year. James Thompson opened Honda's account with his sprint win

LEFT: BOTHWELL PHOTOGRAPHIC. RIGHT: LAT/JEFF BLOXHAM

The series' second ever visit to Croft brought local boy James Thompson his first win of the season and Rickard Rydell a win, an increase in his series lead, and a new reputation as bruising in-fighter. It also thankfully avoided the deluge which had threatened to ruin the previous year's meeting.

It was a day characterised by metal-grinding overtaking moves, with Rydell in the thick of it. Thompson led the sprint all the way from pole to take Honda's first victory of the year, but behind him there was plenty of root and ripple. Thompson's only worry came when a brief shower allowed Nissan's Anthony Reid to close in, but Reid was himself soon under attack from Rydell.

A move at the hairpin was followed by a concerted attempt to re-arrange all the panels on the right-hand side of the Volvo and the left-hand side of the Nissan. Reid held his ground and kept the place, but was prompted to observe: 'Rickard seems to be under a lot of pressure to win the championship. He is driving in a much more robust manner this year.'

Rydell himself was then bundled out of third place by Alain Menu at the hairpin. It was the Renault man's second move - the

first attempt to pass at Tower had been robustly re-buffed by the championship points leader.

In the feature race David Leslie was ahead to start with and looking good even after the pit stops, but he was suffering thanks to an early exit from the sprint. He'd been graunched into the Clervaux gravel and that left him a step behind on set-up. His Primera was now wearing its tyres too hard, whereas others who'd completed the sprint had been able to note the problem and adjust their set-ups.

Rydell had taken the lead with another aggressive move at the hairpin and Leslie's car problems left him unable to respond. By the end Leslie had been all-but caught by his team mate Reid who had moved up from seventh to third and Menu who was fourth, up from ninth.

Menu and Reid were the two making most progress up the standings and although Rydell's points lead had expanded to 42 points, behind him a group of five drivers remained closely packed in the points table with just 11 points covering Alain Menu in second place to Jason Plato in sixth. All of the top six, with good reason, still considered themselves title contenders.

Right: Yorkshire's James Thompson won his first race of the year on his home circuit. Far right: Peugeot had switched engine builders and Harvey and Radisich were smiling, but good results were still elusive. Above: Menu was in fighting form and took a third and a fourth. Above left: Vauxhall's impromptu clothes line

BOTHWELL PHOTOGRAPHIC

LAT/PETER J FOX

ROUND 13	15 LAPS	**ROUND 14**	30 LAPS
DRIVER	**CAR**	**DRIVER**	**CAR**
1 James THOMPSON	Honda Accord	Rickard RYDELL	Volvo S40
2 Anthony REID	Nissan Primera GT	David LESLIE	Nissan Primera GT
3 Alain MENU	Renault Laguna	Anthony REID	Nissan Primera GT
4 Rickard RYDELL	Volvo S40	Alain MENU	Renault Laguna
5 Yvan MULLER	Audi A4	James THOMPSON	Honda Accord
6 John CLELAND	Vauxhall Vectra	Jason PLATO	Renault Laguna
7 Peter KOX	Honda Accord	Gianni MORBIDELLI	Volvo S40
8 Jason PLATO	Renault Laguna	John CLELAND	Vauxhall Vectra
9 Derek WARWICK	Vauxhall Vectra	Will HOY	Ford Mondeo
10 Gianni MORBIDELLI	Volvo S40	Yvan MULLER	Audi A4

Fastest lap James THOMPSON
AUTOSPORT CUP Matt NEAL

Fastest lap David LESLIE
AUTOSPORT CUP Robb GRAVETT

Tested in almost every corner of the country.

Thruxton, Brands Hatch, Silverstone, Snetterton. They're just some of the places y[...]
the A303 in Dorset, or the A686 in Cumbria. No, our motorsport boys haven't decided to indulge [...]

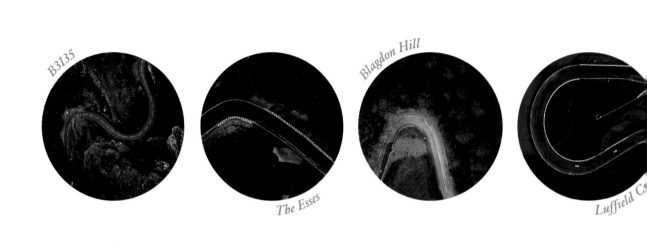

B3135

The Esses

Blagdon Hill

Luffield C[...]

Granted, it's a little less spartan under the skin; there's now air conditioning, sports seats, ABS, and a free op[...]
lowered suspension, 2.5 litre engine, and 16 inch alloys. A word of caution, though. Tempting though it may be to bur[...]

www.vauxhall.co.uk

...d our Vectra SRi V6 24v powering through the bends. Oh, and the B3135 in Somerset,

...ot of illegal road racing. It's just that we've launched a road-going version of the race-bred V6 Challenge car.

ingston Down

Druids Bend

...D player. But outwardly, our V6 SRi has lost little in the way of muscularity, thanks to the stiffened,

...r tarmac, race day antics are best left to the Vectra's more distinguished cousin.

THE VECTRA SRi FROM VAUXHALL

Feel the road.

LEFT: BOTHWELL PHOTOGRAPHIC. RIGHT: LAT/GAVIN LAWRENCE

Thompson dares as Reid spins

James Thompson set up his feature race win at the first corner, which is where Anthony Reid's chance to repeat his sprint race victory went down the drain. Jason Plato, Rickard Rydell and Alain Menu picked up the minor places

Above: Thompson's first corner bravery produced a feature race win. Right: Thommo is joined on the podium by Rydell and Plato

Auto
Trader
Auto
Trader
MICHELIN
MICHELIN
VOLVO
TWR
ERICSSON
James Thompson

Top: Plato challenges winner Reid in the sprint. Above: Rydell hops the kerbs on his way to another big points bag. Right: The midfield battles were full of action

	ROUND 15	17 LAPS	ROUND 16	40 LAPS
	DRIVER	**CAR**	**DRIVER**	**CAR**
1	Anthony REID	Nissan Primera GT	James THOMPSON	Honda Accord
2	Jason PLATO	Renault Laguna	Rickard RYDELL	Volvo S40
3	Alain MENU	Renault Laguna	Jason PLATO	Renault Laguna
4	James THOMPSON	Honda Accord	David LESLIE	Nissan Primera GT
5	Rickard RYDELL	Volvo S40	Yvan MULLER	Audi A4
6	David LESLIE	Nissan Primera GT	Craig BAIRD	Ford Mondeo
7	Gianni MORBIDELLI	Volvo S40	John BINTCLIFFE	Audi A4
8	Will HOY	Ford Mondeo	Will HOY	Ford Mondeo
9	John CLELAND	Vauxhall Vectra	Robb GRAVETT	Honda Accord
10	Derek WARWICK	Vauxhall Vectra	Paul RADISICH	Peugeot 406

Fastest lap Matt NEAL	**Fastest lap** Anthony REID
AUTOSPORT CUP Robb GRAVETT	**AUTOSPORT CUP** Robb GRAVETT

Anthony Reid showed beyond doubt at Snetterton that he and the Nissan had the legs on the rest. Reid took pole for both races and won the sprint, but it all went wrong in the feature when he and Alain Menu clashed at the first corner. Inevitably Rickard Rydell rubbed salt into Reid's wounds by taking home another healthy points bag for second and fifth places.

In the sprint Reid led throughout, despite the attentions of Renault twins Jason Plato and Menu. 'It was a yo-yo scenario,' explained Reid. 'I was quicker on some parts of the circuit, they were quicker at others.' Plato had beaten his team mate away from the line, and it was clear both during and after the race that Menu was not happy playing rear-gunner. Still with the Renault drivers evenly matched in the points, there was no question of team orders being imposed.

Reid held them off to the flag, though he was not entirely happy with his car's balance, saying that it was not as good here at Snetterton as the '97 car had been. Matt Neal rammed the point home by setting the fastest race lap overall in his '97 Primera, although a first lap pit stop to fix a gear linkage problem meant that he was a couple of laps down on the field.

The feature race was effectively decided at the first corner. Reid was comparatively slow away from pole and at Riches it was almost four-abreast. Thompson, on the outside, had made the best start and had the momentum, while Reid was on the inside, and Menu in the middle as Rydell took the sensible option and backed off.

Thompson's situation looked precarious - he'd already noted on the warm-up lap that the outside line was dirty and slippery - but he followed the move through. 'I sent it in, and luckily got round fine,' he explained later. Reid and Menu weren't so lucky, colliding and spinning out as Rydell slinked past. 'I won't tell you what I thought, when they went off, but it was certainly good for the points position,' said the happy Rydell later.

Both Reid and Menu continued, but Reid was pit-bound and Menu got involved in a major shunt with John Cleland. Vauxhall's Scot had lost it at Coram and as he slewed back across the track he was T-boned by Menu, before both cars hit the barrier hard. Menu was OK, but Cleland, who initially had trouble breathing, had cracked some ribs and would miss the next meeting at Thruxton.

Thompson utlimately controlled the race, with Rydell challenging before settling for a lonely second. Plato was third, having beaten off the enthusiastic attempts of David Leslie and Yvan Muller to relieve him of the place.

Above: Derek Warwick's Vectra suffered when a gearbox problem caused a run-in with Matt Neal's Nissan. Left: Reid leads Plato and Menu in the sprint

LAT/GAVIN LAWRENCE

Reid shows his speed

Anthony Reid completely dominated the sprint race for Nissan, but missed out in the feature as Renault's Alain Menu threw in another great drive to to take his third win of the 1998 season

**Left: The crowds
flocked to
Thruxton. Below:
The Williams
team greets Menu
after his feature
win. Bottom: Reid
was an easy
winner in the
sprint**

BOTHWELL PHOTOGRAPHIC

BOTHWELL PHOTOGRAPHIC

BOTHWELL PHOTOGRAPHIC

Anthony Reid confirmed his status as the man of the moment with a dominant win in the sprint, but his challenge again failed to reach its full potential, thanks to pit stop problems. Alain Menu took a fine win in the feature to keep himself in the frame, but that man Rydell was still well in there, quietly racking up points, with two third places.

Reid simply drove away from the pack in the sprint after a rocket-ship start took him past poleman Rydell. 'I couldn't do anything about him,' admitted Menu, who had jumped Rydell on the first lap to take second place and lead the chase.

James Thompson led the rest, short on pace round the entire lap this weekend, but using the Honda's prodigious top speed cannily to defend his position. He held it to the end, but he'd had a busy race, fending off the attentions of first Yvan Muller in the Audi A4 and then - after a Muller sally had gone wrong - Nissan's David Leslie.

Thompson made his presence felt in the feature too. He out-dragged poleman Reid at the start and then again exploited his Accord's strengths to the full to keep the baying pack behind. He managed to keep ahead until the pit stops, then briefly afterwards, but Menu made a top-class move to pass the Honda on the ultra-fast section between Goodwood and Church and take a lead he would hold to the flag.

Thompson looked set to hang onto second place, but gear-selection problems left him vulnerable to the rest and he eventually slipped down to fifth. It was Leslie who eventually took the place, working his way up from sixth early-on. He'd passed Muller before the stops, and made a good move past Rydell at Club after getting the best of a brief dice with team mate Reid and moving past the struggling Thompson into second.

Reid had been Thompson's closest challenger in the early running, but first he had lost time when the engine died in the pits and then he lacked pace thanks to a poor choice of tyres for the second half of the race. He ultimately finished right behind fifth-placed Thompson, with Gianni Morbidelli, in his best race of the season in the Volvo S40, fourth.

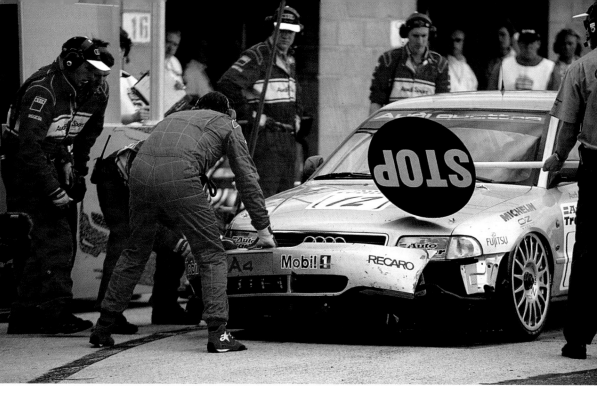

LEFT: LAT/JEFF BLOXHAM. RIGHT: BOTHWELL PHOTOGRAPHIC

LAT/GAVIN LAWRENCE

BOTHWELL PHOTOGRAPHIC

Top left: Neal hunted down Rustad in the sprint. Top right: Muller pits to remove a flapping bumper. Left: Leslie challenges Rydell. Above: Reid on pole for the feature

don't risk it...just ROCK-IT

World Class Freight for Super Touring Types

Delta Way, Egham, Surrey, TW20 8RX

TEL: +44(0)1784 431301 FAX:+44(0)1784 471052

E.Mail: Info@rock-it.co.uk

BOTHWELL PHOTOGRAPHIC

LAT/GAVIN LAWRENCE

BOTHWELL PHOTOGRAPHIC

Top: Will Hoy flies the kerbs. Above: Robb Gravett's Honda Accord lost a wheel, twice. Above right: Reid battles Thompson for the feature race lead

ROUND 17	20 LAPS	**ROUND 18**	35 LAPS
DRIVER	**CAR**	**DRIVER**	**CAR**
1 Anthony REID	Nissan Primera GT	Alain MENU	Renault Laguna
2 Alain MENU	Renault Laguna	David LESLIE	Nissan Primera GT
3 Rickard RYDELL	Volvo S40	Rickard RYDELL	Volvo S40
4 James THOMPSON	Honda Accord	Gianni MORBIDELLI	Volvo S40
5 David LESLIE	Nissan Primera GT	James THOMPSON	Honda Accord
6 Yvan MULLER	Audi A4	Anthony REID	Nissan Primera GT
7 Derek WARWICK	Vauxhall Vectra	Peter KOX	Honda Accord
8 Gianni MORBIDELLI	Volvo S40	John BINTCLIFFE	Audi A4
9 Paul RADISICH	Peugeot 406	Tim HARVEY	Peugeot 406
10 Will HOY	Ford Mondeo	Yvan MULLER	Audi A4

Fastest lap Anthony REID
Autosport Cup Matt NEAL

Fastest lap Anthony REID
Autosport Cup Mark LEMMER

Warwick wins the Fife lottery

It was wet at Knockhill and the rain played a big part in deciding who won the feature. Conditions had been consistent in the sprint and Anthony Reid won, but in the feature it was tyre-choice gamble time. Triple Eight got it right for Derek Warwick, who grabbed his first BTCC win

BOTH PHOTOS: LAT/GAVIN LAWRENCE

Anthony Reid kept up his recent sprint race-winning habit to take his first ever victory on home turf, but it was lottery time in the feature, which went to Vauxhall's Derek Warwick, having been led for a long time by Ford's under-valued Kiwi Craig Baird.

On a consistently wet track, Reid won the sprint comfortably. James Thompson was second despite Yvan Muller's advances. Muller was the star of the race in the Audi. He started sixth, and quickly muscled past David Leslie's Nissan. Menu was his next target and he tested the Renault driver's car control with a biff that sent the Laguna sideways at Butchers. That put Yvan into fourth place behind Peter Kox in the second Honda. Muller wasted no time in spinning the Accord and moving up again.

It was when he tried to oust Thompson that Muller came unstuck. This time the Audi was delayed and Menu sliced past to a third place he held to the flag. Meanwhile Rickard Rydell had been the victim of a first lap accident and failed to finish.

At the start of the feature race the track was dry enough for slick tyres, but rain was in the air. Front-row starter Thompson had a clutch problem and stalled on the line. Behind there was a certain amount of confusion out of which John Cleland's Vectra slewed off into the barrier, knocked off by his own team mate Warwick.

A safety car period ensued while the Vectra was tidied away. During that, light rain started to fall and a handful of drivers stopped for grooved tyres. On the track Reid led the way with Menu in pursuit and the Renault was soon ahead, after tipping Reid's Nissan off the circuit.

As the rain got harder though, the slick-shod runners started to pit and through it all came Baird, who had taken a big gamble to start on intermediates. He was being hunted down by Matt Neal, also on inters and threatening to lift the £100,000 on offer to any Independent to win outright. That dream was soon over though as the rain got harder and Neal slid off.

Baird's lead was not to last either. The track was now so drenched that full wets were the only answer. Warwick had fitted those during the early safety car period, but the rest had to fit theirs while the race was in full flow. Menu lost any chance of a top result when a wheelnut jammed during his stop and, by the time it all settled down, Warwick was well clear.

Muller and Rydell closed the gap over the remaining laps, but Warwick was uncatchable and very happy. 'I've been lucky today,' he admitted, 'but I've worked hard over the last two years and so have Vauxhall and (works team) Triple Eight.

Top: Morbidelli, feature star Baird and Cleland head into the Chicane. Right: Muller was in top form. Above: £100,000 beckoned for Neal, but he slid into the gravel

Audi's dilemma

Yvan Muller notched up his and Audi's best result of the season at Knockhill. Scottish race fans had become used to seeing Audi successes at the Fife circuit, but this year second place was a real triumph, and even that was unexpected.

The A4 quattro had been dominant on the tight little track, winning three of the four races it contested there in 1996 and '97. This season, Muller was certainly worth a place on the podium, but you would have got pretty good odds on him before the race.

The difference is that this year four-wheel drive is gone, banned from Super Touring at manufacturer level, and all competitors were battling on a level playing field. Level, that is, in that all were using front-wheel drive cars, Audi of course was a year or two behind its rivals in gaining experience about how to make a front-driver fly.

By the time the series made its annual visit to

Scotland, Audi Sport UK had made significant progress with the front-drive A4. At Knockhill in the rain, Muller's superb car control and aggression in traffic saw him battling for second in the sprint before finishing fourth and taking that great runner-up slot in the changing conditions of the feature.

The A4's improvement in form continued over the balance of the season and Muller was a regular in the battles at the front of the field in the closing meetings, but at the end of it Audi decided to withdraw from the series. It wanted to promote its quattro technology and, though it had done that this year despite not being able to race a quattro, it felt that would not be an option in the future.

Audi's withdrawal from the series is a shame for the BTCC, but there's no doubt that all-front-drive grids offer simpler, more readily-understood and ultimately more exciting competition.

ROUND 19	22 LAPS		ROUND 20	45 LAPS	
	DRIVER	CAR		DRIVER	CAR
1	Anthony REID	Nissan Primera GT	1	Derek WARWICK	Vauxhall Vectra
2	James THOMPSON	Honda Accord	2	Yvan MULLER	Audi A4
3	Alain MENU	Renault Laguna	3	Rickard RYDELL	Volvo S40
4	Yvan MULLER	Audi A4	4	Alain MENU	Renault Laguna
5	David LESLIE	Nissan Primera GT	5	Jason PLATO	Renault Laguna
6	Will HOY	Ford Mondeo	6	Paul RADISICH	Peugeot 406
7	Peter KOX	Honda Accord	7	Anthony REID	Nissan Primera GT
8	Matt NEAL	Nissan Primera GT	8	Tommy RUSTAD	Renault Laguna
9	Derek WARWICK	Vauxhall Vectra	9	David LESLIE	Nissan Primera GT
10	Paul RADISICH	Peugeot 406	10	John BINTCLIFFE	Audi A4

Fastest lap David LESLIE
AUTOSPORT CUP Matt NEAL

Fastest lap Yvan MULLER
AUTOSPORT CUP Tommy RUSTAD

Tazio Nuvolari was only just over five feet tall, but what he lacked in size he made up for in recklessness. His determination didn't diminish with age, and it received

a test

as stern as any in the 1948 Mille Miglia, when he was fifty six. During the race a crash left his front wing damaged and blocking his view. His solution was to steer his Ferrari straight into a bridge, dislodging the offending metal and allowing him to continue on his way unimpeded. Later in the same race his seat broke, so he commandeered a sack of oranges and lemons to use as a makeshift replacement. Signor Nuvolari was unquestionably a man

# of character.

We're sure he'd have enjoyed a coffee with as intense and distinctive a character as ours.

NESCAFÉ **BLEND ~37~**

A CUP OF CHARACTER

NESCAFÉ BLEND ~37~ **Williams RENAULT**

TITLE SPONSOR OF THE WILLIAMS RENAULT BRITISH TOURING CAR TEAM.

THE DARKER MORE CHARACTERFUL COFFEE FROM NESCAFÉ

Rivals duel for the big prize

The two strongest contenders for the drivers' title were at the heart of the action. Anthony Reid won both races on the road, but the feature was awarded to Rickard Rydell by the stewards

LAT/JEFF BLOXHAM

SUTTON/COLLEY/JAKOB EBREY

With the season reaching its climax, the drivers still in with a chance of catching Rickard Rydell - now just Anthony Reid, Alain Menu and James Thompson - really needed to make progress at Brands Hatch. By the end of the weekend a record crowd had seen Reid give it his best shot and apparently rattle his rival, but ultimately make little headway into Rydell's lead.

Reid won both races on the road, but later lost his first feature race victory in the stewards room, where he was joined by his Swedish rival. Rydell was accused of assaulting Reid after the race and he was found guilty. That sounded serious, but in reality Rydell had just grabbed the Scot's overalls and given him a frank explanation of his attitude to the move Reid had made to gain the lead. His punishment reflected that - not a ban but a big fine (£2000) and

a severe reprimand.

The day had started with considerably more calm. Poleman Reid won the sprint easily from Thompson and Rydell, but the real action was saved for the feature. This time Rydell was on pole and he led away. Reid was immediately all over the back of the Volvo, seeking any possible way past.

He made his move at Druids, giving the S40 a solid belt on the way in. Rydell kept control and it was Reid who came off worse, being forced wide and demoted by Thompson, Menu and Jason Plato.

Reid was not finished yet, though. And he soon battled back into contention. After the pit stops he was second again. He sat behind the Volvo for several laps, before again making his move at Druids. It was another very physical manoeuvre and this time it put him into the lead. That's where he stayed until the chequered flag,

but he was later deemed to have gained an unfair advantage and given a time penalty which bumped him back to second again.

While Reid and Rydell grabbed the headlines, Menu had a solid day on a circuit where his Renault Laguna was no match for the Volvo or Nissan. He was third in the feature and added that to fifth in the sprint to keep at least a mathematical chance of retaining his title. Thompson though was effectively out of it. Second in the sprint was a good start, but when his fourth place on the road in the feature race was turned into ninth by a time penalty for excessive use of the old part of the track at Paddock, the game was up.

Nigel Mansell was on the grid again, but with no rain to help this time he was well out of contention and crashed on the run out of Druids in both races.

LEFT AND PREVIOUS PAGE: LAT/MALCOLM GRIFFITHS

BOTHWELL PHOTOGRAPHIC

Above: Nigel Mansell attracted a record crowd. Left: Guest star Tiff Needell pits the Primera. Top left: Thompson was second in the sprint. Above left: Mansell slams into the barriers

We're right behind
every great British driver.

Swan National is one of the largest fleet providers in the UK. Our daily dealings with both large and small companies have given us an unrivalled understanding of the business car market.

With our range of financial products, dedicated account teams and driver support we provide the added value that companies like yours are looking for from a fleet provider.

Call now for more information: 0500 20 30 30

Swan National
Member HSBC Group

Swan National Limited P.O. Box 5693, 54 Hagley Road Birmingham B16 8PL

PETER J FOX

LEFT & ABOVE: LAT/JEFF BLOXHAM

Top: Leslie
collected an
advertising board.
Above: Neal
celebrates
AUTOSPORT Cup
victory and fifth
overall. Left: Menu
scored well with
fifth and third

Diamond Neal

Matt Neal enjoyed one of his best weekends of the season at Brands Hatch, and for the quickest man in the AUTOSPORT Cup for Independents, that meant a fifth place in the feature and a storming run up from 19th on the grid to ninth in the sprint.

Neal has been the man to prove beyond all doubt that the 1998 rule changes, which guarantee Independents tyre equality with the factory runners and allow significant manufacturer support, allow a well-run and well-driven non-works car to really mix it at the front of the BTCC pack.

This was the third time this year that Neal had brought the Team Dynamics Nissan Primera home in fifth place and he'd produced a number of other top quality performances. He'd set fastest lap overall in the sprint race at Snetterton, been third on the grid for the sprint at Brands earlier in the year and run in third place overall in both sprint and feature.

It's fair to say that Neal had the most competitive equipment of any Independent runner. The Primera was newly-built, to late 1997 specification and over the course of the season it did acquire some updates, but it was never, as team boss Steve Neal was always keen to point out, to full-works '98-spec.

Of the other Independents, both Tommy Rustad in the DC Cook Motorsport Renault Laguna and Robb Gravett in the Rock-It Cargo Honda Accord mixed it with factory cars on several occasions over the course of the season, though they never looked likely to gain podium places except in extraordinary circumstances.

That Neal did on more than one occasion look capable of finishing on the podium overall, meant that there was always the heartening possibility that the £100,000 TOCA had put up for the first Independent to win overall would be awarded...

ROUND 21	30 LAPS	**ROUND 22**	50 LAPS
DRIVER	**CAR**	**DRIVER**	**CAR**
1 Anthony REID	Nissan Primera GT	Rickard RYDELL	Volvo S40
2 James THOMPSON	Honda Accord	Anthony REID	Nissan Primera GT
3 Rickard RYDELL	Volvo S40	Alain MENU	Renault Laguna
4 David LESLIE	Nissan Primera GT	Jason PLATO	Renault Laguna
5 Alain MENU	Renault Laguna	Matt NEAL	Nissan Primera GT
6 Peter KOX	Honda Accord	Yvan MULLER	Audi A4
7 Jason PLATO	Renault Laguna	Peter KOX	Honda Accord
8 John CLELAND	Vauxhall Vectra	Tim HARVEY	Peugeot 406
9 Matt NEAL	Nissan Primera GT	James THOMPSON	Honda Accord
10 Paul RADISICH	Peugeot 406	Paul RADISICH	Peugeot 406

Fastest lap Anthony REID
AUTOSPORT CUP Matt NEAL

Fastest lap Anthony REID
AUTOSPORT CUP Matt NEAL

Reid sets up the big showdown

A win and a second place for Anthony Reid, as Rickard Rydell endured a trying weekend, meant the BTCC gang left the penultimate meeting of the season with the title battle on fire

BOTHWELL PHOTOGRAPHIC

BOTHWELL PHOTOGRAPHIC

BOTHWELL PHOTOGRAPHIC

Far Left: Anthony Reid and the Nissan were top of the pops again. Above left: Warwick Muller and Kox battle. Left: Plato and Muller drench feature-winner Reid

LAT/JEFF BLOXHAM

ROUND 23	20 LAPS	ROUND 24	43 LAPS
DRIVER	**CAR**	**DRIVER**	**CAR**
1 James THOMPSON	Honda Accord	Anthony REID	Nissan Primera GT
2 Anthony REID	Nissan Primera GT	Jason PLATO	Renault Laguna
3 Alain MENU	Renault Laguna	Yvan MULLER	Audi A4
4 David LESLIE	Nissan Primera GT	Rickard RYDELL	Volvo S40
5 Yvan MULLER	Audi A4	Derek WARWICK	Vauxhall Vectra
6 Jason PLATO	Renault Laguna	Will HOY	Ford Mondeo
7 Peter KOX	Honda Accord	Matt NEAL	Nissan Primera GT
8 Will HOY	Ford Mondeo	Tommy RUSTAD	Renault Laguna
9 John CLELAND	Vauxhall Vectra	Gianni MORBIDELLI	Volvo S40
10 Derek WARWICK	Vauxhall Vectra	Tim HARVEY	Peugeot 406

Fastest lap Anthony REID
AUTOSPORT CUP Tommy RUSTAD

Fastest lap James THOMPSON
AUTOSPORT CUP Matt NEAL

Anthony Reid finally took his first feature race win of the season and backed that up with second in the sprint to set up a final meeting showdown with Rickard Rydell, who had a low-scoring weekend. Reid's form also secured the coveted manufacturers' title for Nissan.

After winning five of the previous six sprint races, Reid missed out on this one having been beaten away from pole by James Thompson. Thereafter, though he could shadow the Honda closely, Reid could not find a way past. Alain Menu was third this time, the Renault Laguna now firmly deposed from its position as king of Oulton. Rydell meanwhile had made little progress from a lowly grid slot, which had

SHUTTERSPEED

BOTHWELL PHOTOGRAPHIC

Far left: The Nissans lead the way at the start of the feature race. Left: Two shunts made it another bad day at the office for Paul Radisich

BOTHWELL PHOTOGRAPHIC

Far left: Thompson's Honda sports damage inflicted by Leslie's Nissan. Left: Plato stormed up to second in the feature race. Below left: Reid dominated in the wet qualifying session

been his reward for a mistake during the One-Shot Showdown. He eventually finished out of the points in 11th place.

In the feature race Reid won easily, with Rydell fourth after briefly running in second place thanks to a shunt which put both David Leslie and James Thompson out of the race. Menu was in the wars this time, victim of a three-car accident which was the result of a protracted concertina effect following a mistake by Leslie half a lap earlier. That removed even the mathematical chance Menu had to keep his title bid alive until the final meeting.

Jason Plato took second place with a fine charging drive and Yvan Muller third after a similarly good performance, both of

them moving past Rydell before the end. The Swede was the first to admit that it had not been a good weekend and that there was much work to be done in the week before the finale. 'We knew from the race earlier in the year that we weren't so quick at Oulton Park and we were just too slow today,' said Rydell. Solid performances from Derek Warwick and Will Hoy gave them fifth and sixth places, though neither Vauxhall nor Ford was competitive on the tricky Cheshire track.

Further down the field Tommy Rustad in the DC Cook Motorsport Renault Laguna clinched the AUTOSPORT Cup for Independents with one of the best performances of his first BTCC season.

LAT/JEFF BLOXHAM

Swede as a nut for new king Rickard

It all fell into place perfectly for Rickard Rydell as TWR revived the S40's form. He drove a perfect sprint race to finish second while title rival Anthony Reid faltered. It made Rydell champion with one round left

LEFT: LAT/MALCOLM GRIFFITHS. ABOVE: BOTHWELL PHOTOGRAPHIC

Above: Rydell gives the photographers a champagne bath after clinching the title in the sprint. Left: Menu pits during a bruising last day with Williams Renault

This was the one that mattered, and as qualifying got under way it soon became clear that TWR Racing had done a great job to turn round the Volvo's under-par Oulton Park form and give their man Rickard Rydell everything he needed to defend his points lead. Reid was, as had become the norm over the second half of the season, bang on the pace again and ready to give it his best shot.

Early in the sprint race it looked as though these two would fight out their title battle at the head of the field. Rydell led away from pole and Reid jumped James Thompson mid-way round the first lap to move into a challenging position. Reid moved on to Rydell's tail as he started to think about how to pass, but then he got a bit too close to the Volvo at Copse, lost downforce and had to ease off slightly. 'It was the key moment of the season,' said a thoughtful Reid later. Thompson was still on his tail and grabbed his chance to regain second place. When Reid tried to retaliate at Abbey the pair touched and dropped down the order.

The race was far from over though. An oil lake deposited by AUTOSPORT Cup Honda man Robb Gravett at Becketts brought more chaos and a safety-car period. Rydell's lead vanished, and when the race resumed he was under pressure from Yvan Muller in the Audi and Thompson. Over the next two laps, Thompson shot past both Muller and Rydell on the run between Copse and Becketts. He went on to win for the fourth time this year. Rydell was second and delighted because, with Reid only fifth, that was enough to clinch the drivers' title.

Away from the lead battle Alain Menu and John Cleland renewed the smouldering feud which has flared up from time to time in recent years, swapping paint and bending metal on-track and then letting loose with the verbals afterwards. 'The man's a fool, he thinks he can walk on water,' said Cleland. Menu reckoned the Scot is: 'Past it. He should go home and stay there.'

Reid took a consolation win in the feature, working his way up from fourth on the first lap. His only serious opposition came from team mate and early leader David Leslie. The pair finished the year on a high note for Nissan, with a one-two that secured the teams' title for Vodafone Nissan Racing.

Left: Muller leads a group into Copse. Bottom: David Leslie led the feature and finished second to team mate Reid. Right: Will Hoy drove his last race for the Blue Oval with a 'tache tint. Below right: Kox, Thompson and Menu mix it

LEFT: LAT/MALCOLM GRIFFITHS RIGHT: LAT/PETER J FOX

LAT/PETER J FOX

BOTHWELL PHOTOGRAPHIC

PETER J FOX

LAT/PETER J FOX

Above: Paul Radisich battled with Will Hoy on his way to a fine sixth place in the sprint. Left: Rydell's crew salutes the champion. Right: AUTOSPORT Cup feature race winner Paula Cook.

BOTHWELL PHOTOGRAPHIC

A select band

Paula Cook joined a select band of successful female British touring car racers when she won the AUTOSPORT Cup class in the last race of the season.

The British Formula 3 Championship regular joined the field for the last four rounds, driving a DC Cook Motorsport Honda Accord. At Oulton Park, with next to no testing, she struggled for speed, but a week later at Silverstone her form was much improved and, aided it must be admitted by the problems of her rivals, she won the class.

The last woman to race regularly in the BTCC was Swede Nettan Lindgren — a very competitive driver in the early days of the 2-litre BTCC era with her BMW M3. Lindgren took an excellent 2-litre win at Thruxton in 1990, the series' transitional year from Group A, when she held off a determined last-corner attack from the Rouse Sport Ford Sapphire of double BTCC champion Chris Hodgetts.

Ladies World Rally Champion Louise Aitken-Walker was twice a BTCC class winner with a Vauxhall Astra in 1989. She'd been brought in to support John Cleland's successful championship bid, did just what was required and won when Cleland had problems.

The only other female winner to date was sixties Mini Cooper racer Christabel Carlisle, who took a class win at Goodwood in spring 1962.

Cook's next task is to become a regular Independents' Cup winner during her projected 1999 season and the ultimate ambition must remain to become the first woman to win a BTCC race outright.

ROUND 25	17 LAPS		ROUND 26	30 LAPS	
DRIVER	**CAR**		**DRIVER**	**CAR**	
1	James THOMPSON	Honda Accord	Anthony REID	Nissan Primera GT	
2	Rickard RYDELL	Volvo S40	David LESLIE	Nissan Primera GT	
3	Yvan MULLER	Audi A4	Rickard RYDELL	Volvo S40	
4	Jason PLATO	Renault Laguna	James THOMPSON	Honda Accord	
5	Anthony REID	Nissan Primera GT	Yvan MULLER	Audi A4	
6	Paul RADISICH	Peugeot 406	Jason PLATO	Renault Laguna	
7	Derek WARWICK	Vauxhall Vectra	Peter KOX	Honda Accord	
8	John CLELAND	Vauxhall Vectra	Will HOY	Ford Mondeo	
9	Alain MENU	Renault Laguna	Tommy RUSTAD	Renault Laguna	
10	Will HOY	Ford Mondeo	Derek WARWICK	Vauxhall Vectra	

Fastest lap Anthony REID
AUTOSPORT CUP Mark LEMMER

Fastest lap Rickard RYDELL
AUTOSPORT CUP Paula COOK

LAURENCE BAKER

sh Touring Car Ch
1998

SHUTTERSPEED

Rustad indie end

Tommy Rustad won the AUTOSPORT Cup because of his admirable consistency. Charles Bradley tells the Independent runners' story

As the budgets and technology available to the works teams continued to escalate, the racers in the AUTOSPORT Cup for Independents had their work cut out to keep up with the big boys, but that didn't stop them trying, and some of them from succeeding.

The title was contested by three main protagonists. Tommy Rustad came out on top in his ex-works Renault Laguna, but both Robb Gravett and Matt Neal were formidable opponents.

Rustad's consistency was the key, although he went through a worrying phase of getting involved in accidents during the middle of the season.

The former Renault Spider Eurocup champion had to learn all about front wheel-drive, and all the circuits, in a team that was new to touring cars. Having dropped its F3000 campaign, DC Cook Motorsport ran the Laguna alongside its Formula 3 team and acquitted itself well.

The 30-year-old Norwegian wrapped up the title at the penultimate round at Oulton Park, allowing him to race for the works team at Silverstone. This did his chances of landing a factory drive no harm at all with two solid races - he even had

the audacity to overtake Alain Menu before he was punted off by Vauxhall works man Derek Warwick.

Neal, however, was caught between the devil and the deep blue sea. In the Team Dynamics-run Nissan Primera he had a car which could run on the pace of the works cars, but in doing so, he ran the risk of being taken out.

This happened too many times for him to have any chance of taking the title. Warwick, in particular, was a thorn in his side in the middle of the year and the pair collided on numerous occasions. But the lanky Midlander's numerous appearances in the top five reflected his pace and his ability to race at this level. He deserves a chance in a front-running works car, as he showed with his superb efforts at Bathurst, when he ran recently-crowned BTCC champ Rickard Rydell close for the win.

Reigning champion Gravett continued his efforts to get back into a works seat via the privateers' class. He drove a Brookes Motorsport-run Honda Accord and held the lead of the series for much of the season. But the age of his car worked against him. His car was always high up on the speed trap readings which showed

LAT/GAVIN LAWRENCE

Clockwise from left: Paula Cook joined the Cup for the last four rounds. Robb Gravett and the Honda led the points chase for much of the year. Independents hassled works drivers regularly – this is Matt Neal harrying Ford's Will Hoy. Team Dynamics' graphics were a match for anyone's too. Matt Neal really enjoyed his successes. Champion Rustad leads Neal at Oulton Park

LAT/MALCOLM GRIFFITHS

LAT/JEFF BLOXHAM

SHUTTERSPEED

it lacked the necessary downforce required to compete on a level footing and he couldn't keep pace with the Renault and Nissan in the second half of the year.

Gravett took the runner-up spot by a single point from Neal, even though neither of them finished the last two races due to mechanical failures. It looks unlikely, however, that we will see the former overall champion back behind the wheel in works machinery.

Former VW Vento champion Mark Lemmer finished fourth in his first season in the BTCC. He was loaned a Vectra for his performances in the 1997 Vauxhall Vectra Challenge. At the start of the year it was run by Mint Motorsport but was switched to Mardi Gras Motorsport for the second half. Money was tight, and Lemmer had to miss a few races as a result, but he took two class wins during the season and proved he has the talent to race at this level.

The same couldn't really be said for Roger Moen, who raced a Mardi Gras-run Honda Accord for the first half of the year. The Norwegian and the Honda were consistently the slowest combination in the series but picked up a fair share of points

and Lemmer only just overhauled him at the final round. Moen had long since departed the series as his sponsors pulled out at the halfway point.

Paula Cook took time out from her Formula 3 campaign and contested the last four races of the year in a DC Cook-run Honda Accord. She lucked into a win at the final round and looks set for more next year as her father Derek, who owns the team, is expected to enter a brace of Accords in the 1999 series.

Former champion Lee Brookes appeared at Oulton Park near the end of the year but he didn't complete a racing lap after a cam-belt problem in qualifying. Here is a sadly wasted talent who would be a welcome full-time addition to next year's championship but he just couldn't raise the funds and had to sit the season out.

The prospects for next year look encouraging. Rustad, Neal and Gravett have proved it is possible for independents to mix it with the big boys and a rash of nearly-new Honda Accords look set to join the series with drivers like Vectra Challenge champ Mark Blair and his series nemesis Simon Graves hoping to conclude deals to contest the championship.

FROM F1 TO TOURING CARS AND SPORTSCARS TO RALLY

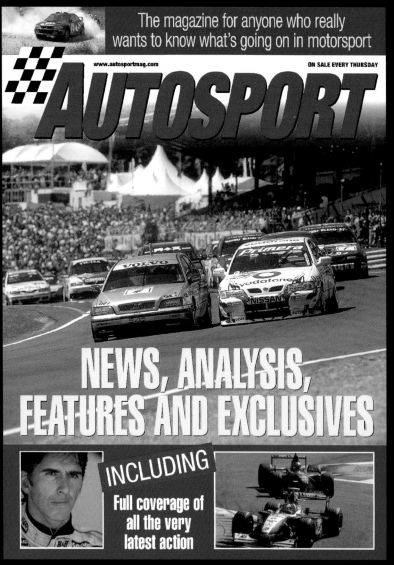

The magazine for anyone who really wants to know what's going on in motorsport

www.autosportmag.com

AUTOSPORT

ON SALE EVERY THURSDAY

NEWS, ANALYSIS, FEATURES AND EXCLUSIVES

INCLUDING

Full coverage of all the very latest action

AUTOSPORT is where the action is, covering every pulsating, high octane, adrenaline pumping incident

On sale every Thursday

www.autosportmag.com

Rustad rules indie roost

Rustad put Norway on the racing map with his AUTOSPORT Cup win, says Charles Bradley

Norway and touring cars are a combination that is about as unlikely as Alf Garnett and Mary Whitehouse.

Other than rallycross king Martin Schanche, the Scandinavian country has had little to cheer motorsport-wise. But Tommy Rustad has done his best to change all that. He scooped the AUTOSPORT Cup for Independents in his first season in the British Touring Car Championship and has raised the nation's awareness of the sport in the process.

'The problem was that it's difficult to find money at home because big companies tend to invest their money in skiing and football,' he says. 'Norway is only a small country and motor racing is very much a new sport there.'

With that hurdle cleared thanks to the support of Renault Sport in France, Rustad had to adjust to the world's premier saloon car championship in the ex-works Laguna. 'I started with a blank piece of paper, so I'm very pleased with how it worked out,' he adds. 'It was very important for me to learn as much as I could this year. I feel that I did that well to win at my first try.'

Rustad is certainly a versatile driver. He

started, predictably, in karts before side-stepping into rallycross. He won the Norwegian title six times, winning 48 races, and then ventured into single-seaters.

The Hakadal resident was a race winner in both Formula Opel and Formula Renault before switching to the Renault Spider Eurocup in 1997, which he won. This year, however, proved to be the 30-year-old's hardest test so far. 'I had to learn about front wheel-drive, all the circuits and the team,' he says. 'DC Cook Motorsport was new to touring cars too, so we all had to learn together.'

After four second places from the first six rounds, he broke his Independents' Cup duck at Brands Hatch in May, before taking a splendid double win at Oulton Park a week later. It was consistent scoring that thwarted his rivals. But Tommy's plans took a big knock, quite literally, at Thruxton in August. He was taken out by a wayward works car, slammed into the barrier, and removed the front of the car.

Team boss Derek Cook was adamant that he'd buy a new bodyshell if it meant keeping Tommy's title effort on course but the car was repaired in time for the next meeting at Knockhill, even if Rustad's

ankle (which he sprained in the accident as his foot snapped the brake pedal in half) was still feeling the after-effects. 'I was worried after Thruxton,' he admits. 'I didn't know if there was enough time to rebuild the car and if there was the budget to do so. The team did an excellent job to fix it, because it was a very big crash.'

He rewarded the team's efforts with a win at Knockhill and then sealed the title one meeting early, giving him the chance to race with the Williams-run works team in the final races at Silverstone.

'Although my main target was always to win the AUTOSPORT Cup, we had hoped to run in the top 10 more often,' he says. 'But when I got in the '98 car I got my answer to why we hadn't been as quick overall as I thought I would be. My best lap at Silverstone was 1.2s faster than my best time in the '97 car.'

That opportunity with the works Renault team gave him a taste of what he's dreamed of ever since: 'My target has always been to get a works seat. There is even more pressure in a works drive and it's important how you work with the team.'

Rustad was impressed by the difference he found at Williams. 'Everyone there just had so much experience,' he says. 'They knew exactly what was happening with the car and had more technology available - everything was a lot more professional.

'The step was much bigger than I expected and, though I didn't get the results I wanted because I got pushed out in both races, I think I performed quite well.'

Now Rustad aims to break into the works driver ranks full-time in 1999. 'I'm determined to try and get something,' he says, 'but it is difficult to get the money side sorted out and there are a lot of drivers on the market. I have some possibilities and I really hope I will be back in the BTCC again.'

Top: Rustad runs the DC Cook Laguna over the kerbs. Above: The Norwegian was not shy about his cultural heritage

BOTH PHOTOS: LAT/JEFF BLOXHAM

From four to two

Audi made good progress as it switched to front-wheel drive, but there were no wins

ENGINE/GEARBOX

TYPE In-line four cylinder, DOHC, 16-valve, alloy block/alloy head
MOUNTING Longitudinal
CAPACITY 1998cc
TRANSMISSION Front-wheel drive Audi longitudinally mounted, sequential-shift gearbox, 6-speed plus reverse

BODY

MODEL Audi A4, 4 door
LENGTH 4479mm
WIDTH 1753mm
HEIGHT 1311mm
WHEELBASE 2619mm
WEIGHT 975kg

SUSPENSION

FRONT Double wishbones, Coilsprings, Gas-filled dampers, Anti-roll bar
REAR Double wishbones, Coilsprings gas-filled dampers, Anti-roll bar
BRAKES Ventilated discs, eight-piston calipers front, two-piston calipers rear
WHEELS 8.2 X 19-inch
TYRES Michelin

This was a tricky year for Audi Sport UK as it fielded the front-wheel drive A4 for the first time, and with less direct support from Audi Sport in Ingolstadt than it had received in the quattro era.

As ever team director John Wickham and team principal Richard Lloyd ran a tight ship. Significant progress was made in the course of the season, and by the closing rounds Yvan Muller was generally a top six runner. He actually took three podium finishes and set fastest lap in the wet at Knockhill, but that elusive first BTCC victory for the front-drive A4 never came. Audi wound up as one of two manufacturers in the championship (from eight) which did not win this year.

The team retained its experienced and effective race-engineering team. Roger King engineered Muller's A4 and Eddie Hinckley linked up with John Bintcliffe. In the past, Audi Sport in Germany had taken charge of all research and development work, but this season all Audi's Super Touring work was put into the hands of one of its lon-term partners - the French firm ROC.

The UK team only ran on official TOCA test days and race weekends and while Muller regularly took part in the ROC development test programmes, Bintcliffe was not often able to test outside TOCA days. That was something which he was not happy about and which appeared to hamper his form.

Engine build and development remained in-house at Audi Sport in Ingolstadt and there were improvements over the course of the season. When new specifications appeared, they went first to Muller, with Bintcliffe's units generally a step behind.

A switch from Dunlop to Michelin tyres over the winter put Audi Sport level with the rest, at least on the rubber front, and Muller, who replaced 1996 champion Frank Biela proved a star, but early in the season the A4 struggled for pace.

One problem seemed to be that the aerodynamic package produced less downforce than those of most of its rivals and even though the engine, certainly initially, was not that powerful, straightline speed was generally good. The car was also prone to high-speed oversteer, something which gave Muller the chance to display all his amazing car-control, but which made the car hard to drive for Bintcliffe, particularly as he was not getting much mileage in the car.

Certainly this was not a season to match the glory days that the team had enjoyed in the previous two years with the quattro and at the end of it Audi UK decided to withdraw from the series.

Its intention, it said, had always been to highlight its technology and particularly its quattro and while it had done that in its marketing and advertising, it felt that without a quattro on-track, the strategy could not continue.

Changing focus

Ford Mondeo Racing's 1998 season was pretty much the same as we've come to expect over the past few years. The new cars arrived late from builder Reynard. Then various problems hampered the efforts of the West Surrey Racing team, which was again charged with running the cars, and drivers Will Hoy, Craig Baird and Nigel Mansell, to string together a decent run of results.

There was certainly more to shout about than in 1996 or 1997 - the car was closer to the pace, guest driver Mansell created much interest and the Mondeo even won a race for the first time since 1995. That was a major highlight - a great win in changeable conditions at Silverstone for Will Hoy.

That was made possible through excellent team work by Dick Bennetts's WSR crew under team manager Malcolm Swetnam, and a superb drive by Will Hoy.

The car also certainly appeared to have a great deal more potential this year. The problem was that it was not brought out. Early in the season, the team had few spares so it could not test and before the season was far-advanced, car builder Reynard cut its links with the project.

Later in the season, Ford decided to move its focus towards its revised 1999 attack with Prodrive. Thereafter development work on the '98 car tailed off - something which clearly disappointed

Mansell when he re-joined the team for rounds 21 and 22 at Brands Hatch.

The result was that there was only a brief period in the middle of the season when serious development work took place, giving WSR's Will Phillips and his engineering team little chance to show what they could do. Needless to say, all the quick teams had been at it since March or before and kept up the momentum throughout the season.

The Mondeo was certainly quick in the wet and Hoy was adamant that it could be in the dry too, if only enough testing time could be found. It was not to be.

And when Ford announced that it was drawing a curtain on its policy of splitting responsibilities between a car builder and a team and joining the majority of manufacturers in the series by entrusting design, build development and the running of the cars to one organisation, - it was soon clear that any hopes of a late run of success were at an end.

WSR had hoped to be given the job, but in the end it went to David Richards' Prodrive organisation, which had recently relinquished the Honda deal.

The good news is that at last a Ford BTCC project appears to be properly under way in good time, and with two of this year's star drivers Alain Menu and Anthony Reid under contract, the Blue Oval must surely have a better season in 1999.

Ford's Mondeo showed promise and Will Hoy won a race, but it was a season of upheavals and no sustained success

ENGINE/GEARBOX

TYPE Six-cylinder, 60 degree Vee, dohc, 24-valve, alloy block/alloy head
MOUNTING Transverse
CAPACITY 2000cc
TRANSMISSION Front-wheel drive Hewland sequential-shift gearbox, 6-speed plus reverse

BODY

MODEL Ford Mondeo 5-door
LENGTH 4556mm
WIDTH 1750mm
HEIGHT 1425mm
WHEELBASE 2704mm
WEIGHT 975kg

SUSPENSION

FRONT MacPherson strut, Lower wishbone, Gas-filled dampers, Anti-roll bar
REAR MacPherson strut, Parallel arms, Forward link, Gas-filled dampers, Anti-roll bar
BRAKES Ventilated discs, six-piston calipers front, four-piston calipers rear
WHEELS 8 X 19-inch
TYRES Michelin

LEFT: BOTHWELL PHOTOGRAPHIC ABOVE: LAT/PETER J FOX. TOP: LAT/MALCOLM GRIFFITHS

The final frontier

If you're searching for the ultimate in braking performance, there's only one name in the universe - **AP Racing**.

AP Racing have been exploring the boundaries of brake and clutch technology for over 50 years. Dedicated to the finest possible standards in design and manufacture, every year our engineers attend over 150 race meetings all over the world.

Ask the people who create the winning cars. In fact, ask the winners of every single F1 Constructors Championship since 1967.

There is only one name when it comes to racing brakes and clutches. Put another way, wherever there's intelligent life, there's **AP Racing**.

RACING

the SCIENCE of FRICTION

AP Racing, Wheler Road, Coventry, CV3 4LB, England. Tel +44 (0)1203 639595 Fax +44 (0)1203 639559

Late chase for pace

Pre-season, Team Honda Sport and its Prodrive-run Hondas were looking forward to a fantastic year. The Banbury outfit's second shot at building a Super Touring Accord looked to be spot-on as James Thompson set the pace in most of the pre-season tests.

However when the serious business started at the opening race meetings, the Accord began to flag. It was soon clear that it was short of pace compared with the front-running Nissans, Volvos and, generally, the Renaults, although Thompson briefly led the points standings after rounds five and six at Donington Park, thanks to some consistent scoring.

The problem seemed to be its low-downforce aerodynamic package. The theory expounded by Thompson pre-season was that the excellent mechanical grip the Accord enjoys, thanks to wishbone suspension all round (a set-up with theoretical advantages which few others enjoy) meant it could be competitive with less downforce.

Combined with Honda's class-leading engine, that should have given the car a significant straight-line speed advantage over the pack, without corresponding problems in the corners.

That proved not to be the case, at least initially, and one could not help but ask if the departure of design team leader Keith Knott (to start his own business) well

before the season began was having its effect. George Howard Chappell was soon recruited to lead the development programme as chief engineer, but vital testing and learning time had been lost.

The team, under the management of Dave Benbow, with Peter Harrison race-engineering Thompson and Spencer Deakin doing the same for Peter Kox, knuckled down and eventually it turned things round. Thompson won four races, but the first was not until the 13th round at Croft.

Thanks to good reliability and some excellent performances from Thompson, the young Yorkshireman remained in contention for the title for much of the season, and moved ahead of defending champion Alain Menu at the final meeting to put himself into third place in the final points table.

Ultimately it was a good season for Honda, but both outside observers and team insiders had expected better before the season started.

In the second half of the year, Thompson was still theoretically in with that chance of winning the championship, but it was an outside chance and Thommo's focus was very much on picking up as many wins as possible to generate publicity for Honda, rather than on formulating a realistic plan to lift the drivers' title.

LAT/JEFF BLOXHAM

Honda won races and Thompson was third in the drivers' points but, pre-season, more had been expected

ENGINE/GEARBOX

TYPE In-line four cylinder, DOHC, 16-valve, alloy block/alloy head
MOUNTING Transverse
CAPACITY 1998cc
TRANSMISSION Front-wheel drive Prodrive/Hewland sequential-shift gearbox, 6-speed plus reverse

BODY

MODEL Honda Accord, 4 door
LENGTH 4685mm
WIDTH 1720mm
HEIGHT 1380mm
WHEELBASE 2720mm
WEIGHT 975kg

SUSPENSION

FRONT Double wishbones, Coilsprings, Gas-filled dampers, Anti-roll bar
REAR Double wishbones, Coilsprings gas-filled dampers, Anti-roll bar
BRAKES Ventilated discs, eight-piston calipers front, two-piston calipers rear
WHEELS 8.2 X 19-inch
TYRES Michelin

LEFT: LAT/GAVIN LAWRENCE. ABOVE: PETER J FOX

WOODCOTE
COPSE
BROOKLANDS
LUFFIELD
PRIORY
MAGGOTTS
BECKETTS
ABBEY
CHAPEL
CLUB
STOWE

for mobile phone coverage
that reaches the furthest corners,
the word is

○ vodafone

Mallock can with a Nissan

Ray Mallock Ltd's second season with Vodafone Nissan Racing was all that it should have been and brought the manufacturers' title, the teams' title and four more wins than any other manufacturer managed.

Ray Mallock's approach was again a hands-on one and by the middle of the season most rivals were prepared to admit that the Nissan was the car to beat. That it was quite such a successful season did not however mean that there were no problems.

By the first race of the season, the programme was not quite as far advanced as everyone wanted and Anthony Reid's own race chassis was only completed just before the first race. Cynical observers were quick to point the finger at the split of design, development and build responsibilities between RML and Nissan Motorsports Europe. NME and its chief engineer Richard Divila held overall responsibility and the design and build brief, but RML was charged with testing, development and running the race team. The team's problems at pit stops early in the year illustrated the problem. Initially there was only enough droop in the suspension to allow the two front wheels to be changed, whereas in many circumstances changing the left-hand side wheels was an advantage. The problem was not solved quickly.

In the end it all worked extremely well, but with a car as good as the '98 Primera there must be team members ruing a missed opportunity - a clean sweep of the titles. If only David Leslie's early-season results could have been added to Anthony Reid's after round six...

Engine problems also played their part early in the year. The top-line works engines, built by John Judd's Engine Developments company were being out-performed by the customer engines, built to late '97 spec by International Engine Services. First Leslie and then Reid switched to IES units and used them for much of the first half of the season, before moving back to the ED units after rounds 13 and 14 at Croft once the problems on those had been sorted.

The team was often reluctant in those early weeks of the season to reveal which engines were in place, with the standard answer from the drivers to the question - 'which engine are you using?', a helpful smile followed by 'a Nissan four-cylinder.'

The bottom line was that the Primera was the car most drivers in the series would have picked this season, given a measure of hindsight and a free choice. And the team, directed by Mallock, managed by Mark Busfield, and with race engineering by Stuart Ayling (Reid) and Phil Barker (Leslie), did a great job this year and carted off its share of the spoils.

Nissan won most races and two titles, but a tentative start to the season denied it the drivers' crown

ENGINE/GEARBOX

TYPE In-line four cylinder, DOHC, 16-valve, alloy block/alloy head
MOUNTING Transverse
CAPACITY 1998cc
TRANSMISSION Front-wheel drive RML/Xtrac sequential-shift gearbox, 6-speed plus reverse

BODY

MODEL Nissan Primera GT, 4 door
LENGTH 4400mm
WIDTH 1700mm
HEIGHT 1395mm
WHEELBASE 2550mm
WEIGHT 975kg

SUSPENSION

FRONT Double wishbones, Coilsprings, Gas-filled dampers, Anti-roll bar
REAR MacPherson strut, Coilsprings gas-filled dampers, Anti-roll bar
BRAKES Ventilated discs, six-piston calipers front, two-piston calipers rear
WHEELS 8 X 19-inch
TYRES Michelin

ALL PHOTOS: BOTHWELL PHOTOGRAPHIC

Esso Ultron

Faster, cleaner protection - right from the start

Lion down, and out

Peugeot's season was a nightmare, bringing few good results and ending in withdrawal from the series after the end of the championship season.

The Esso Ultron Team Peugeot 406s were run for a second season by Motor Sport Developments under managing director David Whitehead. The team was managed by Paul Risbridger, with the design team led by Graeme Garvin. There was also some input from sub-contractor Mike Pilbeam and race engineering was in the hands of Nick Clipson, who worked with Tim Harvey, while Dominic Harlow was teamed with Paul Radisich.

Encouraging pre-season test results for Harvey were not repeated once the racing started and both his car and that of new recruit Radisich soon ran into a rash of engine problems. The motors were losing power and then, more often than not, eventually failing.

Eventually the problem was deemed to be down to flexing engine blocks. What never became entirely clear was whether this was down to metal fatigue on blocks, of which no-one seemed to know the age, or down to the car's design which used the block as a stressed member – something which prompted expressions of surprise from some rival designers...

Once the problem was identified, all angles were covered – new blocks bought in, extra support built into the engine

mounting system, and Peugeot's long-standing engine builder Richard Longman dumped in favour of Mountune.

Reliability did improve thereafter, with almost all retirements after the big changes were implemented prior to round 13, down to contact of one sort or another. But the 406s never caught up in the development race.

All the team's best results eventually came as a result of opportunist drives from Radisich and Harvey, while for much of the season they suffered the indignity of having to chase the quicker AUTOSPORT Cup runners – including Robb Gravett's Honda Accord (which ironically had been built by MSD back in 1996).

Exactly what the worst problem was is unclear. Team sources pointed unerringly at engine problems - lack of reliability in the first part of the season and then lack of development time - whereas Peugeot sources would mention the engine-mounting system and rear suspension problems. Whatever, the final result was the latest in a long line of disappointing seasons for one of the series' stalwarts.

Another bad season in 1999 was not to be contemplated and when Peugeot UK failed to secure the hardware and back-up it felt it needed for 1999 from the French works team, which ran the successful German series 406s, the decision was taken to withdraw.

Peugeot's season was a depressing one. It was the Coventry firm's seventh and proved to be its last

ENGINE/GEARBOX

TYPE In-line four cylinder, DOHC, 16-valve, alloy block/alloy head
MOUNTING Transverse
CAPACITY 1998cc
TRANSMISSION Front-wheel drive MSD/Xtrac, sequential-shift gearbox, 6-speed plus reverse

BODY

MODEL Peugeot 406, 4 door
LENGTH 4546mm
WIDTH 1752mm
HEIGHT 1240mm
WHEELBASE 2668mm
WEIGHT 975kg

SUSPENSION

FRONT MacPherson struts, Coilsprings, Gas-filled dampers, Anti-roll bar
REAR Multi-link trailing arm, MacPherson struts, Coilsprings gas-filled dampers, Anti-roll bar
BRAKES Ventilated discs, 2 x four-piston calipers front, four-piston calipers rear
WHEELS 8.25 X 19-inch
TYRES Michelin

LEFT: PETER J FOX. ABOVE: LAT/GAVIN LAWRENCE. TOP: LAT/JEFF BLOXHAM

Good but not gold

ENGINE/GEARBOX

TYPE In-line four cylinder, DOHC, 16-valve, iron block/alloy head
MOUNTING Transverse
CAPACITY 1998cc
TRANSMISSION Front-wheel drive Williams/Hewland sequential-shift gearbox, 6-speed plus reverse

BODY

MODEL Renault Laguna, 4 door
LENGTH 4508mm
WIDTH 1752mm
HEIGHT 1433mm
WHEELBASE 2670mm
WEIGHT 975kg

SUSPENSION

FRONT MacPherson struts, Coilsprings, Gas-filled dampers, Anti-roll bar
REAR Trailing arm, Torsion bars, Coilsprings, Gas-filled dampers, Anti-roll bar
BRAKES Ventilated discs, six-piston calipers front, four-piston calipers rear
WHEELS 8.3 X 19-inch
TYRES Michelin

Renault's season was a good one, but the title-winning magic of 1997 was missing

Williams and Renault had the unenviable task of sitting on the top of the pile waiting for everyone else to push them off, after the team's fantastic performance in 1997 when they swept all before them.

Under team manager Didier Debae the Didcot outfit did an excellent job again, though, in the end, it failed to retain any of its titles. After another evolutionary re-design, the Laguna, had simply dropped slightly off the pace.

However that wasn't the whole story – things just did not go as smoothly as they had in '97. Lead driver Alain Menu made some mistakes this year, there were also the sort of mishaps which a team on a roll somehow avoids (like Menu's encounter with Paul Radisich at Oulton Park, Plato's exploding disc at Donington and a sticking wheelnut for Menu at Knockhill). But, even without those, they would have been hard-pressed to win the drivers' or manufacturers' titles. Nescafe Blend 37 Williams Renault did remain in contention for the teams' crown right to the end, but, despite fielding a third car for Tommy Rustad, were pipped by Nissan at the Silverstone finale.

The re-design this year was entrusted to Mark Ellis. A stalwart of the team who, as well as being part of the previous design squad under John Russell, had been Menu's race engineer since Williams took over the Laguna programme in 1995. The team were the first to test a full '98-spec car and looked set for another great season.

However the '98 Laguna was not the dominant force its predecessor had been, apparently designed around late-'97 specification Michelin tyres, which were not the same as those supplied this year, and the team had to put up with a merely good season rather than a brilliant one.

Ellis engineered Menu's car for most of the year, before taking a back seat to start work on the 1999 Laguna and then leaving to precede Menu to Ford and Prodrive (where they had first worked together in the 1992 BMW team).

From the seventh meeting of the year at Croft, the well-respected Greg Wheeler was back with the team. He'd engineered Will Hoy at Williams in 1996, before moving with Hoy to Ford and then starting this season with the Mitsubishi World Rally Championship team. Wheeler took over as Menu's engineer, while Jason Plato continued the successful link-up he had forged with Jerry Hughes in 1997.

Engines were as usual built by Sodemo in France and where they had been a major problem in 1996, and a revelation in the 1997 title-winning campaign, this season they were just another effective part of the mix.

It was by no means a bad season and, as you'd expect, Williams were as sharp as anyone in the pits. A more extensive Laguna re-design is now under way for the last year of the current Williams/Renault Super Touring contract.

Winning once more

Triple Eight Race Engineering produced its first in-house Vectra for its second season running the factory Vauxhall Sport programme, and got that winning feeling with three victories - a pair at Donington for John Cleland and one at Knockhill for Derek Warwick.

Indeed for a while it looked as though Cleland might be able to launch a serious bid for the drivers' title. That wasn't to be, with the Vectra only really quick occasionally, but the team can look on this as an excellent consolidation year as it tries to gear up for a seriously successful 1999.

Technical director John Gentry led the design and race engineering strength and at the beginning of the season it was immediately clear that the 1998 Vectra was a great improvement over its unloved predecessors.

In the end the Vectra was only really right on the pace at Donington Park and in the fifth round, Cleland made the very best use of it to win thanks to a superb start from third on the grid. Later in the year, he won again at the Leicestershire track. This time it was slightly less straightforward but Cleland still won the race. It wasn't just any race either, but one that has been hailed as the best ever, and he won it despite dropping down the field at one stage after straying into the Coppice gravel trap.

In the second half of the season Cleland in particular struggled with a car which didn't work its rear tyres hard enough to keep them up to temperature.

Pit work was not a great strength this year. Both drivers regularly lost time in the pits in the first half of the season and Cleland was the only driver all year to be penalised for missing the window during feature races when the mandatory stop must be made.

That mishap was more than off-set by an inspired tyre call during the Knockhill feature race, which set up the team's third win of the year and team director Warwick's first BTCC triumph. He was the first to acknowledge that it had been a team decision, not his own.

A switch of engine builder from Vauxhall's long-term partner Swindon to Opel's builder Spiess reflected a desire to work more closely with the Luton marque's German sister company and there were no complaints on the motor front this year.

On the personnel side, Mark Way engineered Cleland's car all year, while Warwick started off with Dave Kelly, but later worked with Gentry. Team director Ian Harrison moved behind the scenes from mid-season and from that point Paul Hayden took over as team manager.

It was a positive season and there are great hopes for a real championship challenge in 1999.

Vauxhall's second season with Triple Eight brought wins and a much more competitive package

ENGINE/GEARBOX

TYPE In-line four cylinder, DOHC, 16-valve, iron block/alloy head
MOUNTING Transverse
CAPACITY 1998cc
TRANSMISSION Front-wheel drive Xtrac sequential-shift gearbox, 6-speed plus reverse

BODY

MODEL Vauxhall Vectra, 4 door
LENGTH 4477mm
WIDTH 1707mm
HEIGHT 1310mm
WHEELBASE 2640mm
WEIGHT 975kg

SUSPENSION

FRONT MacPherson struts, Lower wishbones, Anti-roll bar
REAR Twin lateral links and trailing arm, Co-axial spring/damper & trailing arm, Anti-roll bar
BRAKES Ventilated discs, six-piston calipers front, four-piston calipers rear
WHEELS 9 X 19-inch
TYRES Michelin

LEFT: BOTHWELL PHOTOGRAPHIC. ABOVE: BOTHWELL PHOTOGRAPHIC. TOP: LAURENCE BAKER

111

100
touring car victories

Michelin Pilots notched up 100 touring car victories by taking the 1998 BTCC title at Silverstone, which neatly coincided with the centenary of Bibendum the Michelin Man. But the ultimate winner is you the motorist. Pilots tested to the limits in the heat of competition ensure you get tyres that excel on the road. Fit the tyres fit for the British Touring Car Champions - Michelin Pilot Sport.

MICHELIN
The more we progress, the further you go.

www.michelin.co.uk

Mission accomplished

BOTHWELL PHOTOGRAPHIC

LEFT: BOTHWELL PHOTOGRAPHIC. TOP: LAURENCE BAKER

This was Tom Walkinshaw Racing, Volvo S40 Racing and Rickard Rydell's year. The S40 was by no means the fastest car everywhere, but it was quickest on some circuits and almost anywhere else it was right up there.

Add in great driving from Rydell and a superb team performance - only Muller's Audi finished more often than Rydell's Volvo, and all Rickard's retirements were down to accidents - and you had a season, which yielded the BTCC's biggest prize – the drivers' title.

Designer Brendan Gribben produced a much-improved second-generation S40, which stunned the opposition at the opening rounds at Thruxton, when Rydell was a full second quicker than the rest in the first qualifying session. From then on it was always one of the cars to beat.

Throughout the year, Rydell and his race engineer Graham Taylor worked well together to produce a competitive car and the team back-up was generally excellent. TWR was one of the teams which got the pit-stops right - both on strategy and speed - from the start of the season.

The new feature race formats gave teams a chance to make a difference and that's exactly what the TWR crew did. Where many outfits seemed to take a handful of races or more to get their heads round the quickest way to complete a pit stop, the men from Leafield were right on it from the very first race. On several occasions this year, Rydell's feature races included immensely valuable, risk-free,

place gains in the pits.

It was a great all-round performance from the TWR Racing team, run as ever by Roger Silman, with team management from Ken Page and engines which were the responsibility of Charlie Bamber at TWR's in-house operation.

The only blot on the copybook was Gianni Morbidelli's poor season and his minimal contribution to the manufacturers' and teams' championship points tallies. The likeable former Grand Prix racer joined up at the beginning of the season, but never really seemed to get to grips with the S40.

Morbidelli's car was engineered by Steve Norris at the beginning of the season and then, after TWR's Nissan Le Mans project was completed, by a refugee from that team – former Renault and Peugeot BTCC engineer Steve Ridgers. The Italian's progress on-track was often spectacular, and the suspicion was that, like many stepping down from powerful single-seaters, he was over-driving the car.

Tom Walkinshaw's firm had originally aimed to produce a championship victory for Volvo in the third year of its relationship. That proved over-optimistic, but this fifth-year success was well-deserved. There are plenty of indications too that TWR are not yet satisfied and an even better season will be sought in 1999. As Rydell said, the S40 was not the best car at the end of the season, so there will be no question of team reclaxation over the winter.

The Volvo S40 and Rickard Rydell were consistent front runners and the Swede a worthy Champion

ENGINE/GEARBOX

TYPE In-line five cylinder, DOHC, 20-valve, alloy block/alloy head
MOUNTING Transverse
CAPACITY 1999cc
TRANSMISSION Front-wheel drive TWR/Xtrac sequential-shift gearbox, 6-speed plus reverse

BODY

MODEL Volvo S40, 4 door saloon
LENGTH 4670mm
WIDTH 1760mm
HEIGHT 1430mm
WHEELBASE 2670mm
WEIGHT 975kg

SUSPENSION

FRONT MacPherson struts, Coilsprings, Gas-filled dampers, Anti-roll bar
REAR Delta-link semi independent, longitudinal trailing arms, Coilsprings Gas-filled dampers, Anti-roll bar
BRAKES Ventilated discs, eight-piston calipers front, two-piston calipers rear
WHEELS 8.2 X 19-inch
TYRES Michelin

DC Cook Motorsport

Title-winning campaign for the DC Cook team, expanding from its single-seater roots. The Yorkshire outfit had an ex-works Laguna and Renault Spider Eurocup Champion Tommy Rustad of Norway in the driving seat.

Over the season, both driver and team, under experienced team manager Paul Haigh, his assistant Ken Clayton and chief engineer Peter Berry (the team also had some engineering advice from Williams) made great progress and consistent scoring brought home the title. The team also did a great job to re-build the Laguna completely after a major shunt at Thruxton, in time for the following meeting at Knockhill. Rustad was rewarded with a run in a works Laguna for the final meeting.

At the end of the season the team also ran Formula 3 racer Paula Cook (daughter of team owner Derek) in a Honda Accord and she won the last round. A two-car Accord team is expected from DCCM in 1999.

Above: Champion Tommy Rustad in the DCCM Laguna leads Mark Lemmer. Right: Paula Cook drove a DCCM Honda in the last four rounds

Team Dynamics

Steve Neal's professional little team followed up its promising performances with a Nissan Primera at the end of 1997, by using the new-shape version this season for Matt Neal.

It was a new car, but built to late '97 specification by Nissan Motorsports Europe and using customer engines from IES. Neal made great use of it.

Steve Neal took on team management responsibilities this season as well as doing much of the engineering work along with race engineer Barry Plowman. The team also used the damper expertise of former ORECA BMW engineer Dave Potter. Added to that, there was some engineering assistance from NME and works team Ray Mallock Ltd. Some updated parts, including the 1998 aerodynamic package, were also supplied during the season.

Three fifth places overall, a fastest lap at Snetterton and some excellent grid places showed just what a good Independent team can manage, and though Neal suffered more than most from the aggression of some of the slower works drivers, and so was only third in the Cup, it was an excellent season overall.

Matt Neal and the Nissan were the fastest combo in the Cup, but run-ins with works cars kept them out of the top two

Rock-It Cargo

Robb Gravett again drove the 1996 Honda Accord he used in 1997, but this time it was run by Brookes Motorsport.

Lee Brookes had not managed to find a budget to compete himself, after two successful seasons with the team in Toyota Carina and Peugeot 406, and so took a major role in running Gravett. He also qualified a second Accord at Oulton in September, but engine problems stopped him racing.

Gravett's car went better than ever and it was often easy to forget that it was a year older than any other car in the AUTOSPORT Cup. Gravett qualified in the top 10 on occasion and finished in the points two times. Ultimately though, his finishing record was not quite consistent enough to let him beat Rustad, he just held onto second place by a point, despite an engine failure in the penultimate round.

Above: Robb Gravett and Brookes Motorsport had the '96 Accord really motoring. Right: Lee Brookes qualified a second Honda at Oulton, but didn't race

ABOVE: SHUTTERSPEED. LEFT: LAT/JEFF BLOXHAM

Mardi Gras Motorsport

Martin Sharpe's Silverstone-based team had a season split between Norwegian Roger Moen's 1997 Honda Accord and Mark Lemmer's Vauxhall Vectra.

The Honda was always well-presented and reliable, but Moen did not get to grips with it and almost always languished at the back of the field. Midway through the season his backers pulled out.

Lemmer then brought his Vectra to the team for several rounds and won at Thruxton.

LEFT: LAT/JEFF BLOXHAM. RIGHT: SHUTTERSPEED

Mint Motorsport

Mint started the season running the Vectra which Vauxhall had loaned to Mark Lemmer as reward for his performances in the 1997 Vauxhall Vectra SRi V6 Challenge.

Lemmer's season started well with a win in the first round at Thruxton, but the performance flattered to deceive. Life became increasingly difficult and then team and car went their separate ways after the mid-season break.

Right: Roger Moen was a regular until July. Above left: Mark Lemmer went well, on occasion

1998 Auto Trader RAC British Touring Car Championship

THRUXTON - APRIL 12-13   ROUNDS 1 & 2

QUALIFYING TIMES - ROUND 1

1	Rickard RYDELL	1:15.603
2	James THOMPSON	1:16.630
3	Jason PLATO	1:16.680
4	Gianni MORBIDELLI	1:16.873
5	Peter KOX	1:17.095
6	David LESLIE	1:17.097
7	John CLELAND	1:17.099
8	Anthony REID	1:17.117
9	Yvan MULLER	1:17.462
10	Paul RADISICH	1:17.494
11	Derek WARWICK	1:17.590
12	Will HOY	1:17.708
13	John BINTCLIFFE	1:17.931
14	Tommy RUSTAD	1:18.136
15	Craig BAIRD	1:19.009
16	Roger MOEN	1:21.101
17	Alain MENU	No time
18	Matt NEAL	No time
19	Mark LEMMER	No time
20	Robb GRAVETT	No time
21	Tim HARVEY	No time

RESULTS - ROUND 1   16 LAPS - 37.70 MILES

	Driver	Car	Race time	Best lap
1	Rickard RYDELL	Volvo S40	21:01.194	1:17.620
2	Jason PLATO	Renault Laguna	21:02.231	1:18.088
3	James THOMPSON	Honda Accord	21:03.020	1:18.022
4	John CLELAND	Vauxhall Vectra	21:08.023	1:18.388
5	Alain MENU	Renault Laguna	21:08.165	1:17.710
6	Gianni MORBIDELLI	Volvo S40	21:08.839	1:18.206
7	David LESLIE	Nissan Primera	21:11.219	1:18.158
8	Anthony REID	Nissan Primera	21:20.533	1:18.385
9	Yvan MULLER	Audi A4	21:23.033	1:18.524
10	Peter KOX	Honda Accord	21:24.013	1:18.328

11 John BINTCLIFFE (Audi A4) 21:24.737, 12 Derek WARWICK (Vauxhall Vectra) 21:25.432, 13 Tim HARVEY (Peugeot 406) 21:38.781, 14 Mark LEMMER (Vauxhall Vectra) 2143.791, 15 Craig BAIRD (Ford Mondeo) 21:47.184, 16 Tommy RUSTAD (Renault Laguna) 22:04.574, 17 Robb GRAVETT (Honda Accord) 22:09.997, 18 Roger MOEN (Honda Accord) 22:10.837
NOT CLASSIFIED Paul RADISICH (Peugeot 406), Will HOY (Ford Mondeo), Matt NEAL (Nissan Primera)

QUALIFYING TIMES - ROUND 2

1	Rickard RYDELL	1:15.786
2	Anthony REID	1:16.182
3	Alain MENU	1:16.345
4	James THOMPSON	1:16.581
5	David LESLIE	1:16.626
6	Jason PLATO	1:16.716
7	John CLELAND	1:16.835
8	Derek WARWICK	1:17.021
9	Peter KOX	1:17.258
10	Paul RADISICH	1:17.415
11	Matt NEAL	1:17.459
12	Tommy RUSTAD	1:17.501
13	Gianni MORBIDELLI	1:17.510
14	Will HOY	1:17.715
15	Mark LEMMER	1:17.728
16	Yvan MULLER	1:18.101
17	Robb GRAVETT	1:18.401
18	Craig BAIRD	1:19.067
19	John BINTCLIFFE	1:20.124
20	Roger MOEN	1:20.148
21	Tim HARVEY	1:36.370

RESULTS - ROUND 2   32 LAPS - 75.39 MILES

		Car	Race time	Best lap
1	Alain MENU	Renault Laguna	42:43.116	1:17.401
2	RICKARD RYDELL	Volvo S40	42:45.716	1:17.557
3	James THOMPSON	Honda Accord	43:23.626	1:18.106
4	Jason PLATO	Renault Laguna	43:26.106	1:17.978
5	Derek WARWICK	Vauxhall Vectra	43:30.009	1:18.510
6	John CLELAND	Vauxhall Vectra	43:32.375	1:18.250
7	Peter KOX	Honda Accord	43:33.453	1:18.753
8	Paul RADISICH	Peugeot 406	43:48.381	1:18.512
9	John BINTCLIFFE	Audi A4	43:56.269	1:18.742
10	Matt NEAL	Nissan Primera	31 laps	1:19.489

11 Gianni MORBIDELLI (Volvo S40) 31 laps, 12 David LESLIE (Nissan Primera) 31 laps, 13 Anthony REID (Nissan Primera) 31 laps, 14 Craig BAIRD (Ford Mondeo) 31 laps, 15 Will HOY (Ford Mondeo) 31 laps, 16 Robb GRAVETT (Honda Accord) 31 laps, 17 Roger MOEN (Honda Accord) 30 laps
NOT CLASSIFIED Yvan MULLER (Audi A4), Mark LEMMER (Vauxhall Vectra), Tim HARVEY (Peugeot 406), Tommy RUSTAD (Renault Laguna)

SILVERSTONE - APRIL 25-26   ROUNDS 3 & 4

QUALIFYING TIMES - ROUND 3

1	James THOMPSON	1:23.859
2	David LESLIE	1:23.943
3	Jason PLATO	1:24.373
4	Gianni MORBIDELLI	1:24.599
5	Derek WARWICK	1:24.600
6	Rickard RYDELL	1:24.617
7	Peter KOX	1:24.736
8	Yvan MULLER	1:25.029
9	Will HOY	1:25.134
10	John CLELAND	1:25.240
11	Matt NEAL	1:25.524
12	Tommy RUSTAD	1:25.549
13	Robb GRAVETT	1:25.550
14	John BINTCLIFFE	1:25.712
15	Tim HARVEY	1:26.096
16	Craig BAIRD	1:26.195
17	Roger MOEN	1:27.458
18	Alain MENU	No time
19	Anthony REID	No time
20	Paul RADISICH	No time
21	Mark LEMMER	No time

RESULTS - ROUND 3   17 LAPS - 36.28 MILES

		Car	Race time	Best lap
1	David LESLIE	Nissan Primera	25:34.057	1:24.576
2	James THOMPSON	Honda Accord	25:40.657	1:25.059
3	Jason PLATO	Renault Laguna	25:41.147	1:24.873
4	Derek WARWICK	Vauxhall Vecta	25:45.175	1:25.552
5	Rickard RYDELL	Volvo S40	25:47.102	1:25.234
6	John CLELAND	Vauxhall Vectra	25:48.469	1:25.456
7	Anthony REID	Nissan Primera	25:51.786	1:25.590
8	Gianni MORBIDELLI	Volvo S40	25:52.224	1:25.467
9	Will HOY	Ford Mondeo	25:56.730	1:25.880
10	Yvan MULLER	Audi A4	25:58.137	1:26.198

11 Tim HARVEY (Peugeot 406) 26:03.164, 12 Paul RADISICH (Peugeot 406) 26:04.118 13 Robb GRAVETT (Honda Accord) 26:05.021, 14 John BINTCLIFFE (Audi A4) 26:05.362, 15 Tommy RUSTAD (Renault Laguna) 26:12.502, 16 Roger MOEN (Honda Accord) 26:44.138
NOT CLASSIFIED Craig BAIRD (Ford Mondeo), Alain MENU (Renault Laguna), Matt NEAL (Nissan Primera), Peter KOX (Honda Accord), Mark LEMMER (Vauxhall Vectra)

QUALIFYING TIMES - ROUND 4

1	Jason PLATO	1:24.948
2	David LESLIE	1:25.157
3	Alain MENU	1:25.699
4	James THOMPSON	1:25.842
5	Yvan MULLER	1:26.129
6	Derek WARWICK	1:26.228
7	Will HOY	1:26.298
8	John CLELAND	1:26.365
9	Peter KOX	1:26.681
10	Tim HARVEY	1:26.753
11	Anthony REID	1:26.839
12	Rickard RYDELL	1:26.907
13	Paul RADISICH	1:26.983
14	Craig BAIRD	1:27.410
15	Matt NEAL	1:28.118
16	Gianni MORBIDELLI	1:28.260
17	John BINTCLIFFE	1:28.309
18	Mark LEMMER	1:28.671
19	Robb GRAVETT	1:29.043
20	Tommy RUSTAD	1:29.408
21	Roger MOEN	1:29.828

RESULTS - ROUND 4   30 LAPS - 67.56 MILES

		Car	Race time	Best lap
1	Will HOY	Ford Mondeo	46:49.868	1:25.893
2	Jason PLATO	Renault Laguna	46:56.735	1:25.196
3	Anthony REID	Nissan Primera	47:01.680	1:26.030
4	Paul RADISICH	Peugeot 406	47:09.811	1:26.011
5	Gianni MORBIDELLI	Volvo S40	47:18.155	1:26.055
6	Derek WARWICK	Vauxhall Vectra	47:59.753	1:25.322
7	John CLELAND	Vauxhall Vectra	48:11.144	1:25.327
8	Yvan MULLER	Audi A4	48:20.213	1:25.548
9	James THOMPSON	Honda Accord	48:23.897	1:24.764
10	Craig BAIRD	Ford Mondeo	29 laps	1:26.063

11 Peter KOX (Honda Accord) 29 laps, 12 Robb GRAVETT (Honda Accord) 29 laps, 13 Tommy RUSTAD (Renault Laguna) 29 laps, 14 Mark LEMMER (Vauxhall Vectra) 29 laps, 15 Roger MOEN (Honda Accord) 29 laps, 16 Matt NEAL (Nissan Primera) 29 laps, 17 John BINTCLIFFE (Audi A4) 29 laps, 18 Tim HARVEY (Peugeot 406) 29 laps
NOT CLASSIFIED Rickard RYDELL (Volvo S40), David LESLIE (Nissan Primera), Alain MENU (Renault Laguna)

DONINGTON PARK - MAY 3-4   ROUNDS 5 & 6

QUALIFYING TIMES - ROUND 5

1 Rickard RYDELL	1:10.170	12 Peter KOX	1:11.331
2 James THOMPSON	1:10.299	13 Will HOY	1:11.378
3 John CLELAND	1:10.592	14 Mark LEMMER	1:11.429
4 Jason PLATO	1:10.709	15 Tim HARVEY	1:11.733
5 Alain MENU	1:10.736	16 John BINTCLIFFE	1:11.747
6 Anthony REID	1:10.827	17 Paul RADISICH	1:11.803
7 David LESLIE	1:11.023	18 Roger MOEN	1:12.882
8 Yvan MULLER	1:11.065	19 Craig BAIRD	1:33.689
9 Derek WARWICK	1:11.068	20 Robb GRAVETT	8:49.830
10 Matt NEAL	1:11.087	21 Gianni MORBIDELLI	No time
11 Tommy RUSTAD	1:11.278		

RESULTS - ROUND 5   18 LAPS - 35.23 MILES

1	John CLELAND	Vauxhall Vectra	21:39.927	1:11.285
2	James THOMPSON	Honda Accord	21:41.415	1:11.300
3	Rickard RYDELL	Volvo S40	21:41.719	1:11.389
4	Alain MENU	Renault Laguna	21:42.232	1:11.327
5	Matt NEAL	Nissan Primera	21:57.633	1:11.925
6	Yvan MULLER	Audi A4	21:58.718	1:12.163
7	Peter KOX	Honda Accord	21:59.015	1:12.100
8	Will HOY	Ford Mondeo	21:59.5671	1:12.324
9	Tim HARVEY	Peugeot 406	22:02.410	1:12.400
10	John BINTCLIFFE	Audi A4	22:03.440	1:11.955

11 Paul RADISICH (Peugeot 406) 22:03.655, 12 Gianni MORBIDELLI (Volvo S40) 22:04.033, 13 Derek WARWICK (Vauxhall Vectra) 22:04.464, 14 Craig BAIRD (Ford Mondeo) 22:13.880, Robb GRAVETT (Honda Accord) 22:17.406, 16 Mark LEMMER (Vauxhall Vectra) 22:17.565, 17 Tommy RUSTAD (Renault Laguna) 17 laps
NOT CLASSIFIED Jason PLATO (Renault Laguna), David LESLIE (Nissan Primera), Anthony REID (Nissan Primera), Roger MOEN (Honda Accord)

QUALIFYING TIMES - ROUND 6

1 David LESLIE	1:10.424	12 Tommy RUSTAD	1:11.360
2 James THOMPSON	1:10.551	13 John BINTCLIFFE	1:11.361
3 Alain MENU	1:10.839	14 Tim HARVEY	1:11.584
4 John CLELAND	1:10.888	15 Robb GRAVETT	1:11.805
5 Anthony REID	1:10.931	16 Mark LEMMER	1:11.990
6 Derek WARWICK	1:10.999	17 Craig BAIRD	1:12.041
7 Matt NEAL	1:11.024	18 Roger MOEN	1:12.690
8 Yvan MULLER	1:11.047	19 Jason PLATO	No time
9 Peter KOX	1:11.186	20 Rickard RYDELL	No time
10 Will HOY	1:11.316	21 Paul RADISICH	No time
11 Gianni MORBIDELLI	1:11.355		

RESULTS - ROUND 6   36 LAPS - 70.45 MILES

1	David LESLIE	Nissan Primera	43:50.894	1:11.494
2	Alain MENU	Renault Laguna	43:57.152	1:11.685
3	John CLELAND	Vauxhall Vectra	44:09.446	1:11.634
4	James THOMPSON	Honda Accord	44:10.294	1:11.946
5	Jason PLATO	Renault Laguna	44:10.680	1:11.851
6	Anthony REID	Nissan Primera	4423.149	1:12.186
7	Rickard RYDELL	Volvo S40	44:23.273	1:11.748
8	Derek WARWICK	Vauxhall Vectra	44:27.820	1:12.047
9	Matt NEAL	Nissan Primera	44:31.026	1:12.253
10	Yvan MULLER	Audi A4	44:34.574	1:12.229

11 Tim HARVEY (Peugeot 406) 44:44.593, 12 Tommy RUSTAD (Renault Laguna) 44:45.635, 13 Craig BAIRD (Ford Mondeo) 44:49.842, 14 John BINTCLIFFE (Audi A4) 44:55.468, 15 Roger MOEN (Honda Accord) 35 laps
NOT CLASSIFIED Will HOY (Ford Mondeo), Mark LEMMER (Vauxhall Vectra), Robb GRAVETT (Honda Accord), Paul RADISICH (Peugeot 406), Peter KOX (Honda Accord), Gianni MORBIDELLI (Volvo S40)

BRANDS HATCH - MAY 16-17   ROUNDS 7 & 8

QUALIFYING TIMES - ROUND 7

1 Rickard RYDELL	45.165	12 Paul RADISICH	46.425
2 Anthony REID	45.364	13 Tommy RUSTAD	46.534
3 Matt NEAL	45.718	14 Craig BAIRD	47.528
4 Will HOY	45.721	15 James THOMPSON	No time
5 Yvan MULLER	45.745	16 David LESLIE	No time
6 Alain MENU	45.757	17 Gianni MORBIDELLI	No time
7 Jason PLATO	45.870	18 Peter KOX	No time
8 John BINTCLIFFE	46.091	19 Mark LEMMER	No time
9 John CLELAND	46.245	20 Tim HARVEY	No time
10 Derek WARWICK	46.363	21 Roger MOEN	No time
11 Robb GRAVETT	46.366		

RESULTS - ROUND 7   25 LAPS - 30.09 MILES

1	Rickard RYDELL	Volvo S40	19:09.833	45.511
2	Anthony REID	Nissan Primera	19:10.492	45.509
3	Alain MENU	Renault Laguna	19:16.671	45.722
4	Jason PLATO	Renault Laguna	19:17.796	45.754
5	Yvan MULLER	Audi A4	19:22.258	45.864
6	John CLELAND	Vauxhall Vectra	19:22.733	45.851
7	Will HOY	Ford Mondeo	19:26.348	45.809
8	Paul RADISICH	Peugeot 406	19:28.414	45.948
9	James THOMPSON	Honda Accord	19:28.973	45.984
10	John BINTCLIFFE	Audi A4	19:29.475	45.927

11 Derek WARWICK (Vauxhall Vectra) 19:32.669, 12 Tommy RUSTAD (Renault Laguna) 19:34.553, 13 Gianni MORBIDELLI (Volvo S40) 19:34.549, 14 Peter KOX (Honda Accord) 19:38.328, 15 Craig BAIRD (Ford Mondeo) 19:41.948, 16 Robb GRAVETT (Honda Accord) 19:43.973, 17 Mark LEMMER (Vauxhall Vectra) 19:51.666, 18 Roger MOEN (Honda Accord) 19:57.113
NOT CLASSIFIED David LESLIE (Nissan Primera), Tim HARVEY (Peugeot 406), Matt NEAL (Nissan Primera)

QUALIFYING TIMES - ROUND 8

1 Rickard RYDELL	44.441	12 Peter KOX	45.305
2 Anthony REID	44.642	13 Tommy RUSTAD	45.310
3 James THOMPSON	44.877	14 Mark LEMMER	45.392
4 Alain MENU	44.890	15 Derek WARWICK	45.397
5 Matt NEAL	44.936	16 Paul RADISICH	45.567
6 David LESLIE	44.959	17 Craig BAIRD	45.616
7 Gianni MORBIDELLI	44.964	18 Tim HARVEY	45.669
8 Yvan MULLER	45.099	19 Robb GRAVETT	45.745
9 Jason PLATO	45.107	20 Will HOY	No time
10 John BINTCLIFFE	45.251	21 Roger MOEN	No time
11 John CLELAND	45.256		

RESULTS - ROUND 8   50 LAPS - 60.18 MILES

1	Rickard RYDELL	Volvo S40	39:17.876	45.811
2	James THOMPSON	Honda Accord	39:20.248	45.774
3	Anthony REID	Nissan Primera	39:20.840	45.677
4	Alain MENU	Renault Laguna	39:28.536	46.097
5	Matt NEAL	Nissan Primera	39:31.068	45.849
6	David LESLIE	Nissan Primera	39:32.056	45.787
7	Peter KOX	Honda Accord	39:41.542	45.982
8	John BINTCLIFFE	Audi A4	39:48.710	46.230
9	John CLELAND	Vauxhall Vectra	39:49.150	46.186
10	Gianni MORBIDELLI	Volvo S40	39:53.136	46.205

11 Tim HARVEY (Peugeot 406) 40:01.181, 12 Paul RADISICH (Peugeot 406) 49 laps, 13 Derek WARWICK (Vauxhall Vectra) 49 laps, 14 Tommy RUSTAD (Renault Laguna) 49 laps, 15 Yvan MULLER (Audi A4) 49 laps, 16 Roger MOEN (Honda Accord) 49 laps, Robb GRAVETT (Honda Accord) 49 laps
NOT CLASSIFIED Craig BAIRD (Ford Mondeo), Will HOY (Ford Mondeo), Jason PLATO (Renault Laguna), Mark LEMMER (Vauxhall Vectra)

OULTON PARK - MAY 24-25   ROUNDS 9 & 10

QUALIFYING TIMES - ROUND 9

1 Alain MENU	59.139	12 Peter KOX	1:00.044
2 Rickard RYDELL	59.187	13 Paul RADISICH	1:00.048
3 James THOMPSON	59.271	14 John BINTCLIFFE	1:00.138
4 David LESLIE	59.374	15 Yvan MULLER	1:00.225
5 Gianni MORBIDELLI	59.442	16 Tim HARVEY	1:00.269
6 Jason PLATO	59.584	17 Craig BAIRD	1:00.856
7 Anthony REID	59.587	18 Robb GRAVETT	1:00.863
8 Matt NEAL	59.716	19 Mark LEMMER	1:00.894
9 John CLELAND	59.808	20 Roger MOEN	1:01.948
10 Will HOY	59.856	21 Tommy RUSTAD	1:37.745
11 Derek WARWICK	1:00.030		

RESULTS - ROUND 9   20 LAPS - 33.08 MILES

1	Alain MENU	Renault Laguna	20:15.790	59.646
2	Rickard RYDELL	Volvo S40	20:18.768	1:00.024
3	David LESLIE	Nissan Primera	20:19.745	1:00.077
4	Jason PLATO	Renault Laguna	20:20.026	59.878
5	Anthony REID	Nissan Primera	20:29.267	59.987
6	Gianni MORBIDELLI	Volvo S40	20:30.206	1:00.128
7	John CLELAND	Vauxhall Vectra	20:31.671	1:00.411
8	Will HOY	Ford Mondeo	20:32.470	1:00.383
9	John BINTCLIFFE	Audi A4	20:33.760	1:00.316
10	Yvan MULLER	Audi A4	20:34.316	1:00.324

11 Derek WARWICK (Vauxhall Vectra) 20:34.944, 12 Paul RADISICH (Peugeot 406) 20:40.671, 13 Tommy RUSTAD (Renault Laguna) 20:41.882, 14 Craig BAIRD (Ford Mondeo) 20:43.091, 15 Robb GRAVETT (Honda Accord) 21:22.013, Roger MOEN (Honda Accord) 19 laps
NOT CLASSIFIED Peter KOX (Honda Accord), James THOMPSON (Honda Accord), Mark LEMMER (Vauxhall Vectra), Tim HARVEY (Peugeot 406), Matt NEAL (Nissan Primera)

QUALIFYING TIMES - ROUND 10

1 Anthony REID	59.122	12 Paul RADISICH	1:00.131
2 Alain MENU	59.150	13 Derek WARWICK	1:00.196
3 David LESLIE	59.313	14 Tommy RUSTAD	1:00.250
4 Jason PLATO	59.470	15 John CLELAND	1:00.284
5 James THOMPSON	59.515	16 Yvan MULLER	1:00.319
6 Rickard RYDELL	59.525	17 Mark LEMMER	1:00.601
7 John BINTCLIFFE	59.830	18 Robb GRAVETT	1:00.766
8 Gianni MORBIDELLI	1:00.036	19 Craig BAIRD	1:00.963
9 Peter KOX	1:00.042	20 Roger MOEN	1:02.489
10 Matt NEAL	1:00.081	21 Tim HARVEY	No time
11 Will HOY	1:00.081		

RESULTS - ROUND 10   40 LAPS - 66.16 MILES

1	Jason PLATO	Renault Laguna	41:20.394	1:00.278
2	Rickard RYDELL	Volvo S40	41:20.974	1:00.449
3	Anthony REID	Nissan Primera	41:21.451	1:00.139
4	Alain MENU	Renault Laguna	41:23.169	1:00.417
5	James THOMPSON	Honda Accord	41:27.320	1:00.747
6	John CLELAND	Vauxhall Vectra	41:40.532	1:00.702
7	Will HOY	Ford Mondeo	41:40.979	1:00.899
8	John BINTCLIFFE	Audi A4	41:43.281	1:00.934
9	Gianni MORBIDELLI	Volvo S40	41:43.867	1:00.396
10	Yvan MULLER	Audi A4	41:44.803	1:00.869

11 Craig BAIRD (Ford Mondeo) 42:09.582, 12 Tommy RUSTAD (Renault Laguna) 42:12.131, 13 Paul RADISICH (Peugeot 406) 42:25.329, 14 Matt NEAL (Nissan Primera) 39 laps, 15 Roger MOEN (Honda Accord) 39 laps, 16 Robb GRAVETT (Honda Accord) 39 laps
NOT CLASSIFIED David LESLIE (Nissan Primera), Derek WARWICK (Vauxhall Vectra), Tim HARVEY (Peugeot 406), Peter KOX (Honda Accord), DNS Mark LEMMER (Vauxhall Vectra)

DONINGTON PARK - JUNE 13-14   ROUNDS 11 & 12

QUALIFYING TIMES - ROUND 11

1	Anthony REID	1:17.618	12	Tommy RUSTAD	1:19.722
2	Rickard RYDELL	1:18.266	13	Gianni MORBIDELLI	1:19.962
3	Nigel MANSELL	1:18.639	14	Matt NEAL	1:20.087
4	David LESLIE	1:18.670	15	Tim HARVEY	1:20.131
5	John CLELAND	1:18.856	16	John BINTCLIFFE	1:20.134
6	Jason PLATO	1:18.868	17	Mark LEMMER	1:20.156
7	James THOMPSON	1:18.878	18	Roger MOEN	1:21.919
8	Will HOY	1:18.909	19	Alain MENU	No time
9	Robb GRAVETT	1:19.194	20	Yvan MULLER	No time
10	Derek WARWICK	1:19.221	21	Paul RADISICH	No time
11	Peter KOX	1:19.530			

RESULTS - ROUND 11   23 LAPS - 45.01 MILES

1	Anthony REID	Nissan Primera	34:23.250	1:18.725
2	Rickard RYDELL	Volvo S40	34:23.955	1:18.664
3	Will HOY	Ford Mondeo	34:24.360	1:19.026
4	Peter KOX	Honda Accord	34:27.922	1:19.465
5	John CLELAND	Vauxhall Vectra	34:29.949	1:18.752
6	Gianni MORBIDELLI	Volvo S40	34:30.488	1:19.540
7	Yvan MULLER	Audi A4	34:31.087	1:19.363
8	Robb GRAVETT	Honda Accord	34:31.438	1:19.660
9	Jason PLATO	Renault Laguna	34:31.661	1:18.766
10	Paul RADISICH	Peugeot 406	34:32.787	1:19.297

DQ Derek WARWICK (Vauxhall Vectra) 34:33.004, 11 Roger MOEN (Honda Accord) 34:43.546, 12 Tommy RUSTAD (Renault Laguna) 34:43.617

NOT CLASSIFIED John BINTCLIFFE (Audi A4), Mark LEMMER (Vauxhall Vectra), Alain MENU (Renault Laguna), James THOMPSON (Honda Accord), David LESLIE (Nissan Primera), Matt NEAL (Nissan Primera), Nigel MANSELL (Ford Mondeo), Tim Harvey (Peugeot 406)

QUALIFYING TIMES - ROUND 12

1	Anthony REID	1:11.005	12	John BINTCLIFFE	1:12.543
2	David LESLIE	1:11.328	13	Yvan MULLER	1:12.565
3	James THOMPSON	1:11.624	14	Matt NEAL	1:12.602
4	Jason PLATO	1:11.662	15	Tim HARVEY	1:12.649
5	Peter KOX	1:11.758	16	Rickard RYDELL	1:13.168
6	John CLELAND	1:12.032	17	Gianni MORBIDELLI	1:13.177
7	Alain MENU	1:12.066	18	Paul RADISICH	1:13.859
8	Will HOY	1:12.174	19	Nigel MANSELL	1:14.042
9	Tommy RUSTAD	1:12.175	20	Mark LEMMER	1:14.680
10	Derek WARWICK	1:12.261	21	Roger MOEN	1:15.608
11	Robb GRAVETT	1:12.438			

RESULTS - ROUND 12   39 LAPS - 76.32 MILES

1	John CLELAND	Vauxhall Vectra	53:49.318	1:14.309
2	David LESLIE	Nissan Primera	53:53.990	1:13.868
3	Derek WARWICK	Vauxhall Vectra	53:57.950	1:14.390
4	Yvan MULLER	Audi A4	54:00.455	1:14.740
5	Nigel MANSELL	Ford Mondeo	54:00.662	1:15.264
6	Matt NEAL	Nissan Primera	54:00.801	1:15.313
7	Gianni MORBIDELLI	Volvo S40	54:45.498	1:14.688
8	Tommy RUSTAD	Renault Laguna	38 laps	1:15.318
9	John BINTCLIFFE	Audi A4	38 laps	1:14.730
10	Roger MOEN	Honda Accord	38 laps	1:17.149

NOT CLASSIFIED Mark LEMMER (Vauxhall Vectra), Anthony REID (Nissan Primera), Jason PLATO (Renault Laguna), James THOMPSON (Honda Accord), Paul RADISICH (Peugeot 406), Peter KOX (Honda Accord), Rickard RYDELL (Volvo S40), Robb GRAVETT (Honda Accord), Will HOY (Ford Mondeo), Alain MENU (Renault Laguna), Tim HARVEY (Peugeot 406)

CROFT - JUNE 27-28   ROUNDS 13 & 14

QUALIFYING TIMES - ROUND 13

1	James THOMPSON	1:21.984	12	Matt NEAL	1:22.928
2	Anthony REID	1:22.076	13	Tim HARVEY	1:23.265
3	Rickard RYDELL	1:22.108	14	Paul RADISICH	1:23.346
4	Yvan MULLER	1:22.179	15	John BINTCLIFFE	1:23.544
5	Peter KOX	1:22.520	16	Tommy RUSTAD	1:23.761
6	David LESLIE	1:22.595	17	Craig BAIRD	1:24.145
7	Alain MENU	1:22.603	18	Roger MOEN	1:24.490
8	Jason PLATO	1:22.637	19	Robb GRAVETT	1:24.946
9	John CLELAND	1:22.663	20	Will HOY	No time
10	Gianni MORBIDELLI	1:22.856	21	Mark LEMMER	No time
11	Derek WARWICK	1:22.865			

RESULTS - ROUND 13   15 LAPS - 31.91 MILES

1	James THOMPSON	Honda Accord	21:01.848	1:22.684
2	Anthony REID	Nissan Primera	21:03.124	1:22.698
3	Alain MENU	Renault Laguna	21:04.694	1:22.910
4	Rickard RYDELL	Volvo S40	21:07.026	1:22.725
5	Yvan MULLER	Audi A4	21:09.541	1:23.580
6	John CLELAND	Vauxhall Vectra	21:09.797	1:23.513
7	Peter KOX	Honda Accord	21:10.651	1:23.657
8	Jason PLATO	Renault Laguna	21:11.001	1:23.588
9	Derek WARWICK	Vauxhall Vectra	21:15.145	1:23.644
10	Gianni MORBIDELLI	Volvo S40	21:15.836	1:23.718

11 Paul RADISICH (Peugeot 406) 21:24.251, 12 Matt NEAL (Nissan Primera) 21:24.437, 13 Will HOY (Ford Mondeo) 21:24.697, 14 Craig BAIRD (Ford Mondeo) 21:27.460, 15 Tommy RUSTAD (Renault Laguna) 21:30.325, 16 Tim HARVEY (Peugeot 406) 21:34.038, 17 Mark LEMMER (Vauxhall Vectra) 14 laps

NOT CLASSIFIED Robb GRAVETT (Honda Accord), John BINTCLIFFE (Audi A4), Roger MOEN (Honda Accord), David LESLIE (Nissan Primera)

QUALIFYING TIMES - ROUND 14

1	David LESLIE	1:22.454	12	Tim HARVEY	1:23.630
2	Rickard RYDELL	1:22.849	13	Matt NEAL	1:23.708
3	Gianni MORBIDELLI	1:22.895	14	Paul RADISICH	1:23.788
4	James THOMPSON	1:22.908	15	John BINTCLIFFE	1:23.939
5	Yvan MULLER	1:23.024	16	Craig BAIRD	1:23.950
6	Peter KOX	1:23.047	17	Will HOY	1:24.048
7	Anthony REID	1:23.108	18	Robb GRAVETT	1:24.160
8	Jason PLATO	1:23.184	19	Tommy RUSTAD	1:24.600
9	Alain MENU	1:23.213	20	Mark LEMMER	1:25.016
10	John CLELAND	1:23.520	21	Roger MOEN	1:25.372
11	Derek WARWICK	1:23.577			

RESULTS - ROUND 14   30 LAPS - 63.81 MILES

1	Rickard RYDELL	Volvo S40	42:30.765	1:22.721
2	David LESLIE	Nissan Primera	42:33.170	1:22.624
3	Anthony REID	Nissan Primera	42:33.921	1:22.818
4	Alain MENU	Renault Laguna	42:34.520	1:23.142
5	James THOMPSON	Honda Accord	42:39.343	1:23.067
6	Jason PLATO	Renault Laguna	42:45.153	1:22.964
7	Gianni MORBIDELLI	Volvo S40	42:47.579	1:22.977
8	John CLELAND	Vauxhall Vectra	42:51.345	1:23.159
9	Will HOY	Ford Mondeo	42:51.346	1:22.834
10	Yvan MULLER	Audi A4	42:55.651	1:23.203

11 John BINTCLIFFE (Audi A4) 43:01.548, 12 Derek WARWICK (Vauxhall Vectra) 43:09.897, 13 Craig BAIRD (Ford Mondeo) 43:12.617, 14 Robb GRAVETT (Honda Accord) 43:26.908, 15 Matt NEAL (Nissan Primera) 43:27.647, 16 Roger MOEN (Honda Accord) 29 laps, 17 Mark LEMMER (Vauxhall Vectra) 29 laps, 18 Tim HARVEY (Peugeot 406) 28 laps

NOT CLASSIFIED
Peter KOX (Honda Accord), Paul RADISICH (Peugeot 406), Tommy RUSTAD (Renault Laguna)

SNETTERTON - JULY 25-26   ROUNDS 15 & 16

QUALIFYING TIMES - ROUND 15

1	Anthony REID	1:08.841	11	Craig BAIRD	1:09.797
2	Alain MENU	1:08.971	12	Tim HARVEY	1:09.818
3	Jason PLATO	1:09.031	13	Derek WARWICK	1:09.895
4	James THOMPSON	1:09.052	14	Will HOY	1:09.950
5	Peter KOX	1:09.156	15	John CLELAND	1:09.979
6	Rickard RYDELL	1:09.189	16	Tommy RUSTAD	1:10.063
7	David LESLIE	1:09.375	17	Robb GRAVETT	1:10.186
8	Gianni MORBIDELLI	1:09.593	18	Paul RADISICH	1:10.538
9	Matt NEAL	1:09.601	19	John BINTCLIFFE	1:10.599
10	Yvan MULLER	1:09.677			

RESULTS - ROUND 15   17 LAPS - 33.18 MILES

1	Anthony REID	Nissan Primera	20:11.954	1:10.389
2	Jason PLATO	Renault Laguna	20:12.434	1:10.504
3	Alain MENU	Renault Laguna	20:12.704	1:10.465
4	James THOMPSON	Honda Accord	20:15.880	1:10.646
5	Rickard RYDELL	Volvo S40	20:16.310	1:10.512
6	David LESLIE	Nissan Primera	20:16.616	1:10.512
7	Gianni MORBIDELLI	Volvo S40	20:23.071	1:10.631
8	Will HOY	Ford Mondeo	20:23.653	1:10.959
9	John CLELAND	Vauxhall Vectra	20:24.369	1:10.973
10	Derek WARWICK	Vauxhall Vectra	20:24.611	1:10.761

11 Craig BAIRD (Ford Mondeo) 20:26.141, 12 Tim HARVEY (Peugeot 406) 20:26.943, 13 Robb GRAVETT (Honda Accord) 20:30.578, 14 John BINTCLIFFE (Audi A4) 20:31.445, 15 Yvan MULLER (Audi A4) 20:34.222, 16 Peter KOX (Honda Accord) 20:34.276, 17 Tommy RUSTAD (Renault Laguna) 20:45.653, 18 Paul RADISICH (Peugeot 406) 20:59.984

NOT CLASSIFIED Matt NEAL (Nissan Primera)

QUALIFYING TIMES - ROUND 16

1	Anthony REID	1:08.792	11	David LESLIE	1:09.351
2	Alain MENU	1:08.815	12	Craig BAIRD	1:09.600
3	James THOMPSON	1:08.841	13	Robb GRAVETT	1:09.724
4	Rickard RYDELL	1:08.874	14	John BINTCLIFFE	1:09.812
5	Jason PLATO	1:08.957	15	Tim HARVEY	1:09.893
6	Yvan MULLER	1:09.156	16	Tommy RUSTAD	1:09.956
7	Peter KOX	1:09.189	17	Will HOY	1:09.969
8	Matt NEAL	1:09.239	18	Paul RADISICH	1:10.160
9	Derekl WARWICK	1:09.322	19	John CLELAND	1:10.201
10	Gianni MORBIDELLI	1:09.346			

RESULTS - ROUND 16   40 LAPS - 78.08 MILES

1	James THOMPSON	Honda Accord	52:37.426	1:10.508
2	Rickard RYDELL	Volvo S40	52:41.761	1:10.524
3	Jason PLATO	Renault Laguna	52:45.833	1:10.777
4	David LESLIE	Nissan Primera	52:46.292	1:10.636
5	Yvan MULLER	Audi A4	52:46.549	1:10.809
6	Craig BAIRD	Ford Mondeo	52:56.152	1:10.917
7	John BINTCLIFFE	Audi A4	53:01.843	1:11.400
8	Will HOY	Ford Mondeo	53:04.956	1:11.272
9	Robb GRAVETT	Honda Accord	53:05.819	1:10.928
10	Paul RADISICH	Peugeot 406	53:08.407	1:11.061

11 Gianni MORBIDELLI (Volvo S40) 53:26.306, 12 Tommy RUSTAD (Renault Laguna) 53:40.383, 13 Matt NEAL (Nissan Primera) 39 laps

NOT CLASSIFIED Anthony REID (Nissan Primera), Tim HARVEY (Peugeot 406), Peter KOX (Honda Accord), Derek WARWICK (Vauxhall Vectra), John CLELAND (Vauxhall Vectra), Alain MENU (Renault Laguna)

THRUXTON - AUGUST 1-2

ROUNDS 17 & 18

QUALIFYING TIMES - ROUND 17

1	Rickard RYDELL	1:15.916	11	Peter KOX	1:17.357
2	Anthony REID	1:16.183	12	Matt NEAL	1:17.520
3	Alain MENU	1:16.377	13	Paul RADISICH	1:17.663
4	Yvan MULLER	1:16.518	14	Will HOY	1:17.742
5	James THOMPSON	1:16.573	15	Robb GRAVETT	1:17.770
6	David LESLIE	1:16.594	16	Tommy RUSTAD	1:17.849
7	Jason PLATO	1:16.635	17	Tim HARVEY	1:18.272
8	Gianni MORBIDELLI	1:16.688	18	Flavio FIGUEIREDO	1:18.394
9	John BINTCLIFFE	1:16.877	19	Craig BAIRD	1:18.427
10	Derek WARWICK	1:17.128	20	Mark LEMMER	1:18.788

RESULTS - ROUND 17 — 20 LAPS - 47.12 MILES

1	Anthony REID	Nissan Primera	29:07.171	1:17.015
2	Alain MENU	Renault Laguna	29:10.659	1:17.327
3	Rickard RYDELL	Volvo S40	29:13.015	1:17.622
4	James THOMPSON	Honda Accord	29:13.726	1:17.377
5	David LESLIE	Nissan Primera	29:14.141	1:17.322
6	Yvan MULLER	Audi A4	29:14.386	1:17.569
7	Derek WARWICK	Vauxhall Vectra	29:15.915	1:17.769
8	Gianni MORBIDELLI	Volvo S40	29:17.323	1:17.248
9	Paul RADISICH	Peugeot 406	29:24.883	1:18.266
10	Will HOY	Ford Mondeo	29:27.809	1:18.007

11 John BINTCLIFFE (Audi A4) 29:28.574, 12 Matt NEAL (Nissan Primera) 29:28.699, 13 Peter KOX (Honda Accord) 29:32.964, 14 Tommy RUSTAD (Renault Laguna) 29:33.682; 15 Tim HARVEY (Peugeot 406) 29:36.328, 16 Robb GRAVETT (Honda Accord) 29:37.559, 17 Flavio FIGUEIREDO (Vauxhall Vectra) 29:37.987, 18 Mark LEMMER (Vauxhall Vectra) 30:04.323
NOT CLASSIFIED Jason PLATO (Renault Laguna), Craig BAIRD (Ford Mondeo)

QUALIFYING TIMES - ROUND 18

1	Anthony REID	1:15.492	11	Tim HARVEY	1:17.075
2	James THOMPSON	1:15.866	12	Matt NEAL	1:17.205
3	Rickard RYDELL	1:16.020	13	Tommy RUSTAD	1:17.273
4	Alain MENU	1:16.058	14	Will HOY	1:17.297
5	Yvan MULLER	1:16.121	15	Paul RADISICH	1:17.331
6	David LESLIE	1:16.216	16	Craig BAIRD	1:17.393
7	John BINTCLIFFE	1:16.621	17	Gianni MORBIDELLI	1:17.593
8	Peter KOX	1:16.842	18	Robb GRAVETT	1:17.698
9	Jason PLATO	1:16.847	19	Flavio FIGUEIREDO	1:18.421
10	Derek WARWICK	1:16.910	20	Mark LEMMER	1:18.758

RESULTS - ROUND 18 — 35 LAPS - 82.46 MILES

1	Alain MENU	Renault Laguna	48:16.489	1:17.847
2	David LESLIE	Nissan Primera	48:18.742	1:17.823
3	Rickard RYDELL	Volvo S40	48:23.664	1:18.056
4	Gianni MORBIDELLI	Volvo S40	48:26.423	1:18.265
5	James THOMPSON	Honda Accord	48:26.544	1:17.759
6	Anthony REID	Nissan Primera	48:27.001	1:17.451
7	Peter KOX	Honda Accord	48:36.514	1:18.263
8	John BINTCLIFFE	Audi A4	48:36.833	1:18.186
9	Tim HARVEY	Peugeot 406	48:41.778	1:18.450
10	Yvan MULLER	Audi A4	48:46.590	1:17.762

11 Flavio FIGUEIREDO (Vauxhall Vectra) 48:50.650, 12 Will HOY (Ford Mondeo) 49:18.586, 13 Mark LEMMER (Vauxhall Vectra) 34 laps
NOT CLASSIFIED Robb GRAVETT (Honda Accord), Jason PLATO (Renault Laguna), Matt NEAL (Nissan Primera), Paul RADISICH (Peugeot 406), Derek WARWICK (Vauxhall Vectra), Tommy RUSTAD (Renault Laguna), DNS Craig BAIRD (Ford Mondeo)

KNOCKHILL - AUGUST 15-16

ROUNDS 19 & 20

QUALIFYING TIMES - ROUND 19

1	Anthony REID	52.509	11	Derek WARWICK	53.744
2	Peter KOX	52.861	12	Tommy RUSTAD	53.751
3	James THOMPSON	52.885	13	Paul RADISICH	53.804
4	David LESLIE	53.040	14	John CLELAND	53.857
5	Alain MENU	53.119	15	Robb GRAVETT	53.871
6	Rickard RYDELL	53.229	16	Tim HARVEY	53.995
7	Yvan MULLER	53.264	17	John BINTCLIFFE	54.006
8	Jason PLATO	53.391	18	Craig BAIRD	54.246
9	Matt NEAL	53.495	19	Gianni MORBIDELLI	58.327
10	Will HOY	53.582			

RESULTS - ROUND 19 — 22 LAPS - 28.60 MILES

1	Anthony REID	Nissan Primera	22:38.846	58.397
2	James THOMPSON	Honda Accord	22:41.040	58.538
3	Alain MENU	Renault Laguna	22:41.687	58.114
4	Yvan MULLER	Audi A4	22:42.038	58.104
5	David LESLIE	Nissan Primera	22:42.496	57.994
6	Will HOY	Ford Mondeo	22:45.585	58.125
7	Peter KOX	Honda Accord	22:46.636	58.349
8	Matt NEAL	Nissan Primera	22:48.223	58.489
9	Derek WARWICK	Vauxhall Vectra	22:52.050	58.747
10	Paul RADISICH	Peugeot 406	22:53.534	58.771

11 Gianni MORBIDELLI (Volvo S40) 22:54.354, 12 Craig BAIRD (Ford Mondeo) 22:54.669, 13 John CLELAND (Vauxhall Vectra) 22:55.390, 14 Tommy RUSTAD (Renault Laguna) 23:05.080, 15 Tim HARVEY (Peugeot 406), 23:33.958
NOT CLASSIFIED
Robb GRAVETT (Honda Accord), John BINTCLIFFE (Audi A4), Jason PLATO (Renault Laguna), Rickard RYDELL (Volvo S40)

QUALIFYING TIMES - ROUND 20

1	Anthony REID	52.465	11	Derek WARWICK	53.538
2	Peter KOX	52.782	12	John CLELAND	53.570
3	James THOMPSON	52.881	13	Paul RADISICH	53.576
4	David LESLIE	52.889	14	Robb GRAVETT	53.588
5	Alain MENU	52.906	15	John BINTCLIFFE	53.618
6	Jason PLATO	52.939	16	Tim HARVEY	53.665
7	Rickard RYDELL	52.992	17	Tommy RUSTAD	53.680
8	Yvan MULLER	53.062	18	Craig BAIRD	53.693
9	Gianni MORBIDELLI	53.083	19	Matt NEAL	No time
10	Will HOY	53.423			

RESULTS - ROUND 20 — 45 LAPS - 58.50 MILES

1	Derek WARWICK	Vauxhall Vectra	47:48.716	59.123
2	Yvan MULLER	Audi A4	47:56.223	57.601
3	Rickard RYDELL	Volvo S40	47:59.444	58.124
4	Alain MENU	Renault Laguna	48:09.168	58.132
5	Jason PLATO	Renault Laguna	48:10.361	57.633
6	Paul RADISICH	Peugeot 406	48:13.073	58.142
7	Anthony REID	Nissan Primera	48:14.746	57.836
8	Tommy RUSTAD	Renault Laguna	48:31.888	58.224
9	David LESLIE	Nissan Primera	48:32.510	57.935
10	John BINTCLIFFE	Audi A4	48:34.737	57.864

11 Tim HARVEY (Peugeot 406) 48:41.651, 12 Robb GRAVETT (Honda Accord) 44 laps, 13 Craig BAIRD (Ford Mondeo) 44 laps, 14 Peter KOX (Honda Accord), 44 laps
NOT CLASSIFIED
Will HOY (Ford Mondeo), Matt NEAL (Nissan Primera), James THOMPSON (Honda Accord), Gianni MORBIDELLI (Volvo S40), John CLELAND (Vauxhall Vectra)

BRANDS HATCH - AUGUST 30-31

ROUNDS 21 & 22

QUALIFYING TIMES - ROUND 21

1	Anthony REID	44.583	12	Tiff NEEDELL	45.391
2	Rickard RYDELL	44.663	13	Tommy RUSTAD	45.425
3	James THOMPSON	44.804	14	Will HOY	45.750
4	David LESLIE	44.998	15	Robb GRAVETT	45.804
5	Alain MENU	45.041	16	Tim HARVEY	45.884
6	Peter KOX	45.046	17	Mark LEMMER	46.088
7	Jason PLATO	45.092	18	Nigel MANSELL	46.219
8	Gianni MORBIDELLI	45.163	19	Matt NEAL	46.577
9	Yvan MULLER	45.321	20	Derek WARWICK	No time
10	Paul RADISICH	45.342	21	John BINTCLIFFE	No time
11	John CLELAND	45.343			

RESULTS - ROUND 21 — 30 LAPS - 36.11 MILES

1	Anthony REID	Nissan Primera	25:31.825	44.967
2	James THOMPSON	Honda Accord	25:34.324	45.336
3	Rickard RYDELL	Volvo S40	25:35.367	45.498
4	David LESLIE	Nissan Primera	25:36.541	45.494
5	Alain MENU	Renault Laguna	25:37.539	45.553
6	Peter KOX	Honda Accord	25:43.246	45.621
7	Jason PLATO	Renault Laguna	25:43.605	45.679
8	John CLELAND	Vauxhall Vectra	25:44.143	45.900
9	Matt NEAL	Nissan Primera	25:44.468	45.578
10	Paul RADISICH	Peugeot 406	25:53.048	46.140

11 Yvan MULLER (Audi A4) 25:53.539, 12 Tiff NEEDELL (Nissan Primera) 25:53.739, 13 John BINTCLIFFE (Audi A4) 25:54.219, 14 Tim HARVEY (Peugeot 406) 25:57.069, 15 Tommy RUSTAD (Renault Laguna) 25:58.888, Robb GRAVETT (Honda Accord) 25:59.646
NOT CLASSIFIED Derek WARWICK (Vauxhall Vectra), Gianni MORBIDELLI (Volvo S40), Will HOY (Ford Mondeo), Mark LEMMER (Vauxhall Vectra), Nigel MANSELL (Ford Mondeo)

QUALIFYING TIMES - ROUND 22

1	Rickard RYDELL	44.300	12	John CLELAND	45.016
2	Anthony REID	44.331	13	Tommy RUSTAD	45.022
3	James THOMPSON	44.567	14	John BINTCLIFFE	45.064
4	Alain MENU	44.609	15	Will HOY	45.087
5	Jason PLATO	44.622	16	Robb GRAVETT	45.101
6	David LESLIE	44.648	17	Tiff NEEDELL	45.110
7	Matt NEAL	44.789	18	Paul RADISICH	45.201
8	Peter KOX	44.795	19	Tim HARVEY	45.401
9	Gianni MORBIDELLI	44.800	20	Nigel MANSELL	45.595
10	Yvan MULLER	44.878	21	Mark LEMMER	45.642
11	Derek WARWICK	44.928			

RESULTS - ROUND 22 — 50 LAPS - 60.18 MILES

1	Rickard RYDELL	Volvo S40	38:54.295	45.618
2	Anthony REID	Nissan Primera	38:54.895	45.040
3	Alain MENU	Renault Laguna	38:56.208	45.457
4	Jason PLATO	Renault Laguna	38:59.488	45.495
5	Matt NEAL	Nissan Primera	39:09.622	45.625
6	Yvan MULLER	Audi A4	39:14.457	45.740
7	Peter KOX	Honda Accord	39:14.778	45.803
8	Tim HARVEY	Peugeot 406	39:22.999	45.844
9	James THOMPSON	Honda Accord	39:28.452	45.289
10	Paul RADISICH	Peugeot 406	39:28.579	45.201

11 John BINTCLIFFE (Audi A4) 39:29.112, 12 Robb GRAVETT (Honda Accord) 39:29.360, 13 Tommy RUSTAD (Renault Laguna) 39:38.604, 14 Derek WARWICK (Vauxhall Vectra) 39:57.845, Tiff NEEDELL (Nissan Primera) 49 laps, 16 Mark LEMMER (Vauxhall Vectra) 49 laps
NOT CLASSIFIED Will HOY (Ford Mondeo), Nigel MANSELL (Ford Mondeo), Gianni MORBIDELLI (Volvo S40), David LESLIE (Nissan Primera), John CLELAND (Vauxhall Vectra)

OULTON PARK - SEPTEMBER 12-13

ROUNDS 23 & 24

QUALIFYING TIMES - ROUND 23

1	Anthony REID	59.032
2	James THOMPSON	59.200
3	Alain MENU	59.235
4	David LESLIE	59.289
5	Yvan MULLER	59.457
6	Jason PLATO	59.574
7	Peter KOX	59.601
8	Gianni MORBIDELLI	59.695
9	Matt NEAL	59.889
10	John CLELAND	1:00.075
11	Tommy RUSTAD	1:00.094
12	Will HOY	1:00.179
13	Robb GRAVETT	1:00.298
14	John BINTCLIFFE	1:00.368
15	Tim HARVEY	1:00.393
16	Derek WARWICK	1:00.626
17	Paul RADISICH	1:00.819
18	Lee BROOKES	1:01.588
19	Rickard RYDELL	1:01.769
20	Paula COOK	1:01.911

RESULTS - ROUND 23 — 20 LAPS - 33.08 MILES

1	James THOMPSON	Honda Accord	20:21.174	59.913
2	Anthony REID	Nissan Primera	20:21.686	59.629
3	Alain MENU	Renault Laguna	20:22.519	59.948
4	David LESLIE	Nissan Primera	20:23.431	59.868
5	Yvan MULLER	Audi A4	20:24.346	1:00.217
6	Jason PLATO	Renault Laguna	20:29.147	1:00.272
7	Peter KOX	Honda Accord	20:31.756	1:00.147
8	Will HOY	Ford Mondeo	20:32.402	1:00.426
9	John CLELAND	Vauxhall Vectra	20:32.714	1:00.560
10	Derek WARWICK	Vauxhall Vectra	20:35.350	1:00.562

11 Rickard RYDELL (Volvo S40) 20:35.920, 12 Tommy RUSTAD (Renault Laguna) 20:39.735, 13 Matt NEAL (Nissan Primera) 20:40.838, 14 Tim HARVEY (Peugeot 406) 20:42.856, 15 Robb GRAVETT (Honda Accord) 20:52.718, 16 Paula COOK (Honda Accord) 21:17.602
NOT CLASSIFIED Paul RADISICH (Peugeot 406), John BINTCLIFFE (Audi A4), Gianni MORBIDELLI (Volvo S40), DNS Lee BROOKES (Honda Accord)

QUALIFYING TIMES - ROUND 24

1	Anthony REID	1:05.982
2	David LESLIE	1:06.193
3	Rickard RYDELL	1:06.442
4	Yvan MULLER	1:06.541
5	Derek WARWICK	1:06.680
6	James THOMPSON	1:06.698
7	John CLELAND	1:06.746
8	Jason PLATO	1:06.798
9	Alain MENU	1:06.885
10	Robb GRAVETT	1:06.927
11	Paul RADISICH	1:06.995
12	Will HOY	1:07.095
13	Gianni MORBIDELLI	1:07.145
14	Tommy RUSTAD	1:07.334
15	John BINTCLIFFE	1:07.336
16	Tim HARVEY	1:07.969
17	Peter KOX	1:07.979
18	Lee BROOKES	1:08.499
19	Paula COOK	1:09.376
20	Matt NEAL	No time

RESULTS - ROUND 24 — 43 LAPS - 71.12 MILES

1	Anthony REID	Nissan Primera	45:25.368	59.686
2	Jason PLATO	Renault Laguna	45:33.114	1:00.050
3	Yvan MULLER	Audi A4	45:35.037	59.913
4	Rickard RYDELL	Volvo S40	45:39.576	1:00.088
5	Derek WARWICK	Vauxhall Vectra	45:42.940	1:00.328
6	Will HOY	Ford Mondeo	45:49.890	1:00.408
7	Matt NEAL	Nissan Primera	45:56.918	1:00.219
8	Tommy RUSTAD	Renault Laguna	45:59.190	1:00.580
9	Gianni MORBIDELLI	Volvo S40	46:10.774	1:00.519
10	Tim HARVEY	Peugeot 406	46:16.135	1:00.720

11 John CLELAND (Vauxhall Vectra) 42 laps, 12 Robb GRAVETT (Honda Accord) 42 laps, 13 Paula COOK (Honda Accord) 41 laps
NOT CLASSIFIED Peter KOX (Honda Accord), James THOMPSON (Honda Accord), David LESLIE (Nissan Primera), Alain MENU (Renault Laguna), Paul RADISICH (Peugeot 406), John BINTCLIFFE (Audi A4), DNS Lee BROOKES (Honda Accord)

SILVERSTONE - SEPTEMBER 19-20

ROUNDS 25 & 26

QUALIFYING TIMES - ROUND 25

1	Rickard RYDELL	1:23.364
2	James THOMPSON	1:23.421
3	Anthony REID	1:23.579
4	Yvan MULLER	1:23.592
5	Alain MENU	1:23.671
6	Peter KOX	1:23.814
7	David LESLIE	1:23.983
8	Will HOY	1:24.176
9	Gianni MORBIDELLI	1:24.272
10	Derek WARWICK	1:24.340
11	Jason PLATO	1:24.446
12	Matt NEAL	1:24.891
13	John BINTCLIFFE	1:24.964
14	Paul RADISICH	1:25.115
15	John CLELAND	1:25.245
16	Nigel MANSELL	1:25.376
17	Robb GRAVETT	1:25.573
18	Mark LEMMER	1:26.252
19	Paula COOK	1:26.492
20	Tommy RUSTAD	1:28.007
21	Tim HARVEY	1:34.997

RESULTS - ROUND 25 — 17 LAPS - 38.28 MILES

1	James THOMPSON	Honda Accord	26:16.080	1:24.612
2	Rickard RYDELL	Volvo S40	26:18.273	1:25.006
3	Yvan MULLER	Audi A4	26:19.922	1:25.076
4	Jason PLATO	Renault Laguna	26:20.104	1:25.027
5	Anthony REID	Nissan Primera	26:24.568	1:24.556
6	Paul RADISICH	Peugeot 406	26:29.588	1:25.643
7	Derek WARWICK	Vauxhall Vectra	26:32.291	1:25.027
8	John CLELAND	Vauxhall Vectra	26:36.123	1:25.469
9	Alain MENU	Renault Laguna	26:38.024	1:25.162
10	Will HOY	Ford Mondeo	26:38.848	1:25.992

11 Tommy RUSTAD (Renault Laguna) 26:40.078, 12 John BINTCLIFFE (Audi A4) 26:40.702, 13 David LESLIE (Nissan Primera) 26:41.497, 14 Nigel MANSELL (Ford Mondeo) 26:43.184, 15 Mark LEMMER (Vauxhall Vectra) 26:44.527, 16 Paula COOK (Honda Accord) 26:58.670, 17 Gianni MORBIDELLI (Volvo S40) 27:01.895
NOT CLASSIFIED Peter KOX (Honda Accord), Robb GRAVETT (Honda Accord), Tim HARVEY (Peugeot 406), Matt NEAL (Nissan Primera)

QUALIFYING TIMES - ROUND 26

1	David LESLIE	1:23.628
2	Yvan MULLER	1:23.804
3	James THOMPSON	1:23.955
4	Anthony REID	1:24.069
5	Rickard RYDELL	1:24.089
6	Peter KOX	1:24.186
7	Alain MENU	1:24.286
8	Jason PLATO	1:24.292
9	Gianni MORBIDELLI	1:24.347
10	Paul RADISICH	1:24.401
11	Tommy RUSTAD	1:24.436
12	Will HOY	1:24.750
13	John BINTCLIFFE	1:24.939
14	Derek WARWICK	1:24.996
15	John CLELAND	1:25.025
16	Tim HARVEY	1:25.167
17	Matt NEAL	1:25.222
18	Nigel MANSELL	1:25.430
19	Robb GRAVETT	1:25.990
20	Mark LEMMER	1:26.253
21	Paula COOK	1:27.000

RESULTS - ROUND 26 — 30 LAPS - 67.56 MILES

1	Anthony REID	Nissan Primera	43:30.180	1:24.907
2	David LESLIE	Nissan Primera	43:32.490	1:24.931
3	Rickard RYDELL	Volvo S40	43:33.022	1:24.904
4	James THOMPSON	Honda Accord	43:38.539	1:25.175
5	Yvan MULLER	Audi A4	43:41.662	1:25.210
6	Jason PLATO	Renault Laguna	43:43.527	1:25.035
7	Peter KOX	Honda Accord	43:50.079	1:25.325
8	Will HOY	Ford Mondeo	44:01.548	1:25.943
9	Tommy RUSTAD	Renault Laguna	44:13.858	1:25.643
10	Derek WARWICK	Vauxhall Vectra	44:23.926	1:25.443

11 Nigel MANSELL (Ford Mondeo) 44:27.272, 12 Paula COOK (Honda Accord) 29 laps, 13 Mark LEMMER (Vauxhall Vectra) 29 laps, 14 Paul RADISICH (Peugeot 406) 27 laps
NOT CLASSIFIED Matt NEAL (Nissan Primera), John CLELAND (Vauxhall Vectra), Alain MENU (Renault Laguna), Gianni MORBIDELLI (Volvo S40), Tim HARVEY (Peugeot 406), John BINTCLIFFE (Audi A4), DNS Robb GRAVETT (Honda Accord)

FINAL CHAMPIONSHIP POINTS

DRIVERS

1	Rickard RYDELL	254
2	Anthony REID	239
3	James THOMPSON	203
4	Alain MENU	187
5	Jason PLATO	163
6	David LESLIE	148
7	Yvan MULLER	110
8	John CLELAND	106
9	Derek WARWICK	70
10	Will HOY	69
11	Gianni MORBIDELLI	56
12	Peter KOX	52
13	Matt NEAL	35
14	Paul RADISICH	31
15	John BINTCLIFFE	23
16	Tommy RUSTAD	12
17	Tim HARVEY	10
18	Nigel MANSELL	7
	Robb GRAVETT	7
20	Craig BAIRD	6
21	Roger MOEN	1

BOTHWELL

AUTOSPORT CUP

1	Tommy RUSTAD	251
2	Robb GRAVETT	212
3	Matt NEAL	211
4	Mark LEMMER	95
5	Roger MOEN	92
6	Paula COOK	27

MANUFACTURERS

1	Nissan	273
2	Volvo	245
3	Renault	244
4	Honda	222
5	Vauxhall	162
6	Audi	150
7	Ford	117
8	Peugeot	96

TEAMS

1	Vodafone Nissan Racing	168
2	Blend 37 Williams Renault	159
3	Volvo S40 Racing	140
4	Team Honda Sport	95
5	Vauxhall Sport	75
6	Audi Sport UK	59
7	Ford Mondeo Racing	44
8	Team Dynamics Max Power	24
9	Esso Ultron Team Peugeot	19

LAURENCE RAVEN

PA, AUDIO & VISUAL SERVICES FOR ALL
APPLICATIONS - CONFERENCES, EVENTS,
PRODUCTIONS, LAUNCHES, SPORTING FIXTURES
AND PERMANENT VENUES.

EVENT TECHNICAL SERVICES

EVENT TECHNICAL SERVICES FROM THE
PROVISION OF A SINGLE GENERATOR TO A
COMPLETE PACKAGE FOR A CORPORATE
HOSPITALITY VILLAGE.

RADIO

SPECIAL EVENT MOBILE RADIO STUDIOS
COMPLETE WITH AM/FM TRANSMISSION.

AVAILABLE FROM STOCK
INDOOR PA SYSTEMS
OUTDOOR PA SYSTEMS
TWO WAY RADIO
RADIO MICROPHONES
COMMENTARY VEHICLES
DOUBLE DECKER CONTROL UNITS
HOSPITALITY TV
VIDEO SYSTEMS
SATELLITE SYSTEMS
VIDEO AND FILM PROJECTION
VIDEO RECORDING
VIDEO WALL
AUDIO VISUAL PRODUCTION
EVACUATION PA SYSTEM
CHANDELIERS
DECORATIVE LIGHTING
UTILITY LIGHTING
BROADCAST CAMERA FACILITIES
TV AND VIDEO PRODUCTION
DRIVE-IN VIDEO STUDIO
IN-HOUSE EDITING
RESEARCH AND SCRIPT WRITING
MEETING PRESENTATION
CONFERENCE PRESENTATION
EVENT RADIO STATION
MOBILE RADIO VEHICLES
SUPERSILENT GENERATORS
MODULAR POWER DISTRIBUTION
COOLING/HEATING EQUIPMENT
FIRE ALARMS
FIRE EXTINGUISHERS
TIMING EQUIPMENT
ENGINEERS AND TECHNICIANS
PAT TESTING
16TH EDITION TESTING

THE STUDIO,
OVERTHORPE ROAD,
BANBURY,
OXON OX16 8SX
TEL: 01295 262000
FAX: 01295 271386
ON SITE SILVERSTONE
TEL: 01327 858269
ON SITE NAC STONELEIGH
TEL: 01203 417733

Who won what?

Touring car racing enjoyed another strong year, with Super Touring the most popular formula from Australia to Europe to South America

HALL/SUTTON

Some of the most spectacular touring car racing of the 1998 season came in Australia where the mighty Supercar V8 Holdens and Fords never failed to excite. And they were more than just a loud noise, with champion Craig Lowndes showing how wild they could be. Right: German champion Johnny Cecotto leads at the Nurburgring

AUSTRALIAN TOURING CAR CHAMPIONSHIP

FEBRUARY 1 — SANDOWN
1 John Bowe — Ford Falcon
2 Craig Lowndes — Holden Commodore
3 Glenn Seton — Ford Falcon
4 Steven Richards — Holden Commodore
5 Larry Perkins — Holden Commodore
6 Jason Bargwanna — Holden Commodore

1 Craig Lowndes — Holden Commodore
2 John Bowe — Ford Falcon
3 Glenn Seton — Ford Falcon
4 Russell Ingall — Holden Commodore
5 Larry Perkins — Holden Commodore
6 Mark Skaife — Holden Commodore

1 Craig Lowndes — Holden Commodore
2 Russell Ingall — Holden Commodore
3 Glenn Seton — Ford Falcon
4 John Bowe — Ford Falcon
5 Larry Perkins — Holden Commodore
6 Dick Johnson — Ford Falcon

FEBRUARY 8 — SYMMONS PLAIN
1 Glenn Seton — Ford Falcon
2 Mark Skaife — Holden Commodore
3 Craig Lowndes — Holden Commodore
4 Russell Ingall — Holden Commodore
5 Jason Bargwanna — Holden Commodore
6 Dick Johnson — Ford Falcon

1 Craig Lowndes — Holden Commodore
2 Mark Skaife — Holden Commodore
3 Russell Ingall — Holden Commodore
4 Jason Bargwanna — Holden Commodore
5 Jason Bright — Ford Falcon
6 Larry Perkins — Holden Commodore

1 Craig Lowndes — Holden Commodore
2 Mark Skaife — Holden Commodore
3 Jason Bargwanna — Holden Commodore
4 Jason Bright — Ford Falcon
5 Larry Perkins — Holden Commodore
6 Russell Ingall — Holden Commodore

MARCH 29 — LAKESIDE
1 John Bowe — Ford Falcon
2 Dick Johnson — Ford Falcon
3 Russell Ingall — Holden Commodore
4 Larry Perkins — Holden Commodore
5 Tony Longhurst — Ford Falcon
6 Craig Lowndes — Holden Commodore

1 Russell Ingall — Holden Commodore
2 Dick Johnson — Ford Falcon
3 Larry Perkins — Holden Commodore
4 Craig Lowndes — Holden Commodore
5 Tony Longhurst — Ford Falcon
6 Jason Bright — Ford Falcon

1 Russell Ingall — Holden Commodore
2 Dick Johnson — Ford Falcon
3 Larry Perkins — Holden Commodore
4 Craig Lowndes — Holden Commodore
5 Tony Longhurst — Ford Falcon
6 Steven Richards — Holden Commodore

APRIL 19 — PHILLIP ISLAND
1 Mark Skaife — Holden Commodore
2 Craig Lowndes — Holden Commodore
3 Russell Ingall — Holden Commodore
4 Glenn Seton — Ford Falcon
5 Jason Bright — Ford Falcon
6 John Bowe — Ford Falcon

1 Craig Lowndes — Holden Commodore
2 Mark Skaife — Holden Commodore
3 Russell Ingall — Holden Commodore
4 Glenn Seton — Ford Falcon
5 John Bowe — Ford Falcon
6 Jason Bright — Ford Falcon

1 Russell Ingall — Holden Commodore
2 Craig Lowndes — Holden Commodore
3 John Bowe — Ford Falcon
4 Larry Perkins — Holden Commodore
5 Tony Longhurst — Ford Falcon
6 Alan Jones — Ford Falcon

MAY 3 — WINTON
1 Russell Ingall — Holden Commodore
2 John Bowe — Ford Falcon
3 Larry Perkins — Holden Commodore
4 Craig Lowndes — Holden Commodore
5 Tony Longhurst — Ford Falcon
6 Mark Skaife — Holden Commodore

1 John Bowe — Ford Falcon
2 Russell Ingall — Holden Commodore
3 Craig Lowndes — Holden Commodore
4 Larry Perkins — Holden Commodore
5 Mark Skaife — Holden Commodore
6 Tony Longhurst — Ford Falcon

1 John Bowe — Ford Falcon
2 Mark Skaife — Holden Commodore
3 Russell Ingall — Holden Commodore
4 Tony Longhurst — Ford Falcon
5 Dick Johnson — Ford Falcon
6 Paul Romano — Holden Commodore

MAY 24 — MALLALA
1 John Bowe — Ford Falcon
2 Russell Ingall — Holden Commodore
3 Craig Lowndes — Holden Commodore
4 Larry Perkins — Holden Commodore
5 Dick Johnson — Ford Falcon
6 Steven Johnson — Holden Commodore

1 Russell Ingall — Holden Commodore
2 Dick Johnson — Ford Falcon
3 Craig Lowndes — Holden Commodore
4 Glenn Seton — Ford Falcon
5 Jason Bright — Ford Falcon
6 John Faulkner — Holden Commodore

1 Craig Lowndes — Holden Commodore
2 Russell Ingall — Holden Commodore
3 Glenn Seton — Ford Falcon
4 Steven Johnson — Holden Commodore
5 Jason Bright — Ford Falcon
6 Jason Bargwanna — Holden Commodore

MAY 31 — BARBAGALLO
1 Craig Lowndes — Holden Commodore
2 Mark Skaife — Holden Commodore

3 Russell Ingall — Holden Commodore
4 Dick Johnson — Ford Falcon
5 Larry Perkins — Holden Commodore
6 Glenn Seton — Ford Falcon

1 Craig Lowndes — Holden Commodore
2 Mark Skaife — Holden Commodore
3 Russell Ingall — Holden Commodore
4 Larry Perkins — Holden Commodore
5 Dick Johnson — Ford Falcon
6 Jason Bright — Ford Falcon

1 Craig Lowndes — Holden Commodore
2 Russell Ingall — Holden Commodore
3 Mark Skaife — Holden Commodore
4 Larry Perkins — Holden Commodore
5 John Faulkner — Holden Commodore
6 Jason Bargwanna — Holden Commodore

JUNE 21 — CALDER PARK
1 Craig Lowndes — Holden Commodore
2 Mark Skaife — Holden Commodore
3 Jason Bright — Ford Falcon
4 Jason Bargwanna — Holden Commodore
5 Glenn Seton — Ford Falcon
6 Garth Tander — Holden Commodore

1 Jason Bargwanna — Holden Commodore
2 Craig Lowndes — Holden Commodore
3 Jason Bright — Ford Falcon
4 Russell Ingall — Holden Commodore
5 Mark Skaife — Holden Commodore
6 Glenn Seton — Ford Falcon

JULY 19 — HIDDEN VALLEY
1 Craig Lowndes — Holden Commodore
2 Mark Skaife — Holden Commodore
3 Mark Larkham — Ford Falcon
4 Tony Longhurst — Ford Falcon
5 Paul Romano — Holden Commodore
6 Glenn Seton — Ford Falcon

1 Russell Ingall — Holden Commodore
2 Jason Bargwanna — Holden Commodore
3 Tony Longhurst — Ford Falcon
4 Paul Romano — Holden Commodore
5 Glenn Seton — Ford Falcon
6 Larry Perkins — Holden Commodore

1 Russell Ingall — Holden Commodore
2 Jason Bargwanna — Holden Commodore
3 Glenn Seton — Ford Falcon
4 Larry Perkins — Holden Commodore
5 Mark Larkham — Ford Falcon
6 Craig Lowndes — Holden Commodore

AUGUST 2 — ORAN PARK
1 Craig Lowndes — Holden Commodore
2 Mark Skaife — Holden Commodore
3 Jason Bright — Ford Falcon
4 Tony Longhurst — Ford Falcon
5 Glenn Seton — Ford Falcon
6 Russell Ingall — Holden Commodore

1 Craig Lowndes — Holden Commodore
2 Mark Skaife — Holden Commodore
3 Jason Bargwanna — Holden Commodore
4 Tony Longhurst — Ford Falcon
5 Glenn Seton — Ford Falcon
6 Garth Tander — Holden Commodore

1 Craig Lowndes — Holden Commodore
2 Mark Skaife — Holden Commodore
3 Jason Bargwanna — Holden Commodore
4 Paul Romano — Holden Commodore
5 Tony Longhurst — Ford Falcon
6 Garth Tander — Holden Commodore

CHAMPIONSHIP POSITIONS
1	Craig Lowndes	992
2	Russell Ingall	942
3	Mark Skaife	768
4	Larry Perkins	722
5	John Bowe	682
6	Glenn Seton	676

AUSTRALIAN SUPER TOURING CHAMPIONSHIP

APRIL 5 — CALDER PARK
1 Cameron McConville — Audi A4
2 Cameron McLean — BMW 320i
3 Brad Jones — Audi A4
4 Jim Richards — Volvo S40
5 Mark Adderton — Honda Accord
6 Peter Hills — Ford Mondeo

1 Cameron McConville — Audi A4
2 Brad Jones — Audi A4
3 Cameron McLean — BMW 320i
4 Jim Richards — Volvo S40
5 Mark Adderton — Honda Accord
6 Bob Tweedie — Vauxhall Cavalier

APRIL 26 — ORAN PARK
1 Brad Jones — Audi A4
2 Cameron McConville — Audi A4
3 Jim Richards — Volvo S40
4 John Henderson — Opel Vectra
5 Trevor Sheumach — BMW 318i
6 Ron Searle — Toyota Camry

1 Brad Jones — Audi A4
2 Cameron McConville — Audi A4
3 Jim Richards — Volvo S40
4 Cameron McLean — BMW 320i
5 Mark Adderton — Honda Accord
6 Ron Searle — Toyota Camry

MAY 17 — PHILLIP ISLAND
1 Cameron McConville — Audi A4
2 Jim Richards — Volvo S40
3 Cameron McLean — BMW 320i
4 Mark Adderton — Honda Accord
5 Troy Searle — BMW 318i
6 Peter Hills — Ford Mondeo

1 Jim Richards — Volvo S40
2 Brad Jones — Audi A4
3 Cameron McLean — BMW 320i
4 Cameron McConville — Audi A4
5 Mark Adderton — Honda Accord
6 Troy Searle — BMW 318i

JUNE 7 — EASTERN CREEK
1 Jim Richards — Volvo S40
2 Brad Jones — Audi A4
3 Cameron McConville — Audi A4
4 Cameron McLean — BMW 320i
5 Mark Adderton — Honda Accord
6 Ron Searle — Toyota Camry

1 Brad Jones — Audi A4
2 Jim Richards — Volvo S40
3 Troy Searle — BMW 318i
4 Jim Matthews — BMW 318i
5 Ron Searle — Toyota Camry
6 Adam Kaplan — Nissan Primera

JUNE 28 — LAKESIDE
1 Brad Jones — Audi A4
2 Cameron McConville — Audi A4
3 Jim Richards — Volvo S40
4 Cameron McLean — BMW 320i
5 Mark Adderton — Honda Accord
6 David Auger — Alfa Romeo 155

1 Brad Jones — Audi A4
2 Cameron McLean — BMW 320i
3 Jim Richards — Volvo S40
4 Mark Adderton — Honda Accord
5 Peter Hills — Ford Mondeo
6 Ron Searle — Toyota Camry

JULY 19 — MALLALA
1 Brad Jones — Audi A4
2 Cameron McConville — Audi A4
3 Cameron McLean — BMW 320i
4 Jim Richards — Volvo S40
5 Peter Hills — Ford Mondeo
6 Bob Tweedie — Vauxhall Cavalier

1 Cameron McConville — Audi A4
2 Brad Jones — Audi A4
3 Cameron McLean — BMW 320i
4 Jim Richards — Volvo S40
5 Peter Hills — Ford Mondeo
6 Adam Kaplan — Nissan Primera

AUGUST 9 — WINTON
1 Cameron McConville — Audi A4
2 Jim Richards — Volvo S40
3 Cameron McLean — BMW 320i
4 Mark Adderton — Honda Accord
5 Peter Hills — Ford Mondeo
6 Anthony Robson — BMW 318i

1 Cameron McConville — Audi A4
2 Cameron McLean — BMW 320i
3 Jim Richards — Volvo S40
4 Brad Jones — Audi A4
5 Mark Adderton — Honda Accord
6 Peter Hills — Ford Mondeo

AUGUST 30 — ORAN PARK
1 Cameron McConville — Audi A4
2 Brad Jones — Audi A4
3 Cameron McLean — BMW 320i
4 Jim Richards — Volvo S40
5 Peter Hills — Ford Mondeo
6 Mark Adderton — Honda Accord

1 Brad Jones — Audi A4
2 Cameron McLean — BMW 320i
3 Cameron McConville — Audi A4
4 Trevor Sheumach — Audi A4
5 Mark Zonneveld — Ford Mondeo
6 Peter Hills — Ford Mondeo

CHAMPIONSHIP POSITIONS
1	Brad Jones	190
2	Cameron McConville	184

DPPI/THIERRY DELAUNAY

3 Jim Richards 163
4 Cameron McLean 142
5 Mark Adderton 79
6 Peter Hills 70

BELGIAN PROCAR CHAMPIONSHIP

APRIL 19 ZOLDER
1 Vincent Radermecker Peugeot 306
2 Sebastien Ugeux Peugeot 306
3 Thierry Tassin Honda Integra
4 Pierre-Yves Corthals Renault Megane
5 Frederic Moreau BMW 320i
6 Didier Defourny BMW 320i

1 Sebastien Ugeux Peugeot 306
2 Vincent Radermecker Peugeot 306
3 Thierry Tassin Honda Integra
4 Duncan Huisman BMW 320i
5 Pierre-Yves Corthals Renault Megane
6 Patrick Simons Renault Megane

MAY 3 SPA
1 Stephane de Groodt Honda Integra
2 Sebastien Ugeux Peugeot 306
3 Philippe Tollenaire Honda Integra
4 Grant Elliott Honda Integra
5 Frederic Moreau BMW 320i
6 Bart Ide Renault Megane

1 Stephane de Groodt Honda Integra
2 Sebastien Ugeux Peugeot 306
3 Thierry Tassin Honda Integra
4 Vincent Radermecker Peugeot 306
5 Grant Elliott Honda Integra
6 Duncan Huisman BMW 320i

MAY 31 ZOLDER
1 Thierry Tassin Honda Integra
2 Vincent Radermecker Peugeot 306
3 Sebastien Ugeux Peugeot 306
4 Stephane de Groodt Honda Integra
5 Pierre-Yves Corthals Renault Megane
6 Duncan Huisman BMW 320i

1 Thierry Tassin Honda Integra
2 Vincent Radermecker Peugeot 306
3 Sebastien Ugeux Peugeot 306
4 Pierre-Yves Corthals Renault Megane
5 Duncan Huisman BMW 320i
6 Patrick Slaus BMW 320i

JUNE 14 SPA
1 Pierre-Yves Corthals/Kurt Mollekens Renault Megane
2 Thierry Tassin/Philippe Favre Honda Integra
3 Vanina Ickx/Franck Lagorce Renault Megane
4 Duncan Huisman/Patrick Huisman BMW 320i
5 Fred Bouvy/Kurt Thiers BMW 320i
6 Alain Cudini/Pierre Fermine BMW 320i

JULY 4/5 SPA
1 Alain Cudini/Marc Duez/Eric van de Poele BMW 320i
2 Sebastien Ugeux/Jean Vanderwauwer/Max Weisenburger Peugeot 306
3 Pierre-Yves Corthals/Franck Lagorce/Kurt Mollekens Renault Megane
4 Pierre Fermine/Alain Ferte/David Saelens BMW 320i
5 Eric Bachelart/Stephane de Groodt/Didier Defourny Honda Integra
6 Jacques Laffite/Pierre van Vliet/Pascal Witmeur Peugeot 306

AUGUST 9 CHIMAY
1 Vincent Radermecker Peugeot 306
2 Pierre-Yves Corthals Renault Megane
3 Grant Elliott Honda Integra
4 Sebastien Ugeux Peugeot 306
5 Stephane de Groodt Honda Integra
6 Vincent Vosse Nissan Primera

1 Vincent Radermecker Peugeot 306
2 Grant Elliott Honda Integra
3 Stephane de Groodt Honda Integra
4 Dirk Schoysman Nissan Primera
5 Thierry Tassin Honda Integra
6 Frederic Moreau BMW 320i

SEPTEMBER 27 SPA
1 Thierry Tassin Honda Integra
2 Sebastien Ugeux Peugeot 306
3 Vincent Vosse Nissan Primera
4 Stephane de Groodt Honda Integra
5 Pierre-Yves Corthals Renault Megane
6 Grant Elliott Honda Integra

1 Thierry Tassin Honda Integra
2 Stephane de Groodt Honda Integra
3 Grant Elliott Honda Integra
4 Dirk Schoysman Nissan Primera
5 Vanina Ickx Renault Megane
6 Bart Ide Peugeot 306

OCTOBER 11 ZOLDER
1 Stephane de Groodt Honda Integra
2 Vincent Vosse Nissan Primera
3 Sebastien Ugeux Peugeot 306
4 Bart Ide Peugeot 306
5 Pierre-Yves Corthals Renault Megane
6 Thierry Tassin Honda Integra

1 Sebastien Ugeux Peugeot 306
2 Thierry Tassin Honda Integra
3 Stephane de Groodt Honda Integra
4 Vincent Radermecker Peugeot 306
5 Vincent Vosse Nissan Primera
6 Bart Ide Peugeot 306

CHAMPIONSHIP POSITIONS
1 Sebastien Ugeux 218
2 Thierry Tassin 188
3 Stephane de Groodt 174
4 Pierre-Yves Corthals 160
5 Vincent Radermecker 157
6 Grant Elliott 116

DUTCH TOURING CAR CHAMPIONSHIP

CHAMPIONSHIP POSITIONS
1 Donald Molenaar (Renault Megane) 149
2 Sandor van Es (BMW 320i) 137
3 Allard Kalff (Mitsubishi Carisma) 129
4 Marcel Alderden (Renault Megane) 113
Duncan Huisman (BMW 320i) 113
6 Frans Verschuur (Renault Megane) 107

FINNISH TOURING CAR CHAMPIONSHIP

CHAMPIONSHIP POSITIONS
1 Arto Salmenautio (BMW 320i) 354
2 Olli Haapalainen (VW Golf GTi) 327
3 Toni Rouokonen (Honda Integra) 325
4 Matti Alamaki (BMW 320i) 303
5 Markus Palttala (Honda Integra) 263
6 Aarne Mustonen (BMW 320i) 256

FRENCH TOURING CAR CHAMPIONSHIP

MARCH 29 LEDENON
1 Marcel Tarres Ford Mondeo
2 Carlo Lusser Toyota Carina
3 Christophe Dechavanne Audi 80
4 Johnny Hauser Toyota Carina
5 Norbert Zehnder Peugeot 405
6 Etienne Casubolo BMW 320i

1 Christophe Dechavanne Audi 80
2 Johnny Hauser Toyota Carina
3 Carlo Lusser Toyota Carina
4 Eric Cayrolle BMW 320i
5 Marcel Tarres Ford Mondeo
6 Norbert Zehnder Peugeot 405

APRIL 13 NOGARO
1 Jan Nilsson Volvo S40
2 Christophe Dechavanne Audi 80
3 Eric Cayrolle BMW 320i
4 Patrick Herbert Opel Vectra
5 Etienne Casubolo BMW 320i
6 Carlos Antunes Tavares Renault Megane

1 Eric Cayrolle BMW 320i
2 Christophe Dechavanne Audi 80
3 Marcel Tarres Ford Mondeo
4 Jan Nilsson Volvo S40
5 Carlos Antunes Tavares Renault Megane
6 Yvan Lebon BMW 320i

MAY 3 MAGNY-COURS
1 Christophe Dechavanne Audi 80
2 Eric Cayrolle BMW 320i
3 Patrick Herbert Opel Vectra
4 Pierre Hirschi Opel Vectra
5 Bruno Hernandez BMW 320i
6 Daniel Josseron Opel Vectra

1 Eric Cayrolle BMW 320i
2 James Ruffier Opel Vectra
3 Christophe Dechavanne Audi 80
4 Gilles Duqueine BMW 320i
5 Michel Bandura Peugeot 405
6 Carlos Antunes Tavares Renault Megane

MAY 17 DIJON-PRENOIS
1 Eric Cayrolle BMW 320i
2 James Ruffier Opel Vectra
3 Norbert Zehnder Peugeot 405
4 Carlo Lusser Toyota Carina
5 Pierre Hirschi Opel Vectra
6 Daniel Bandura Peugeot 405

1 Eric Cayrolle BMW 320i
2 Christophe Dechavanne Audi 80
3 Daniel Josseron Opel Vectra
4 Carlo Lusser Toyota Carina
5 Patrick Herbert Opel Vectra
6 Ernst Wiedmer Peugeot 405

JUNE 1 PAU
1 Eric Cayrolle BMW 320i
2 Christophe Dechavanne Audi 80
3 Bruno Hernandez BMW 320i
4 Carlos Antunes Tavares Renault Megane
5 Yvan Lebon BMW 320i
6 Laurent Devesa Peugeot 405

1 Eric Cayrolle BMW 320i
2 Christophe Dechavanne Audi 80
3 Bruno Hernandez BMW 320i
4 Carlos Antunes Tavares Renault Megane
5 Willy Maljean BMW 320i
6 Yvan Lebon BMW 320i

JUNE 14 CHARADE
1 Christophe Dechavanne Audi 80
2 Eric Cayrolle BMW 320i
3 Pierre Hirschi Opel Vectra
4 Elviar Fehlman Toyota Carina
5 Carlos Antunes Tavares Renault Megane
6 Yvan Lebon BMW 320i

1 Eric Cayrolle BMW 320i
2 Carlo Lusser Toyota Carina
3 Christophe Dechavanne Audi 80
4 Pierre Hirschi Opel Vectra
5 Daniel Josseron Opel Vectra
6 Patrick Herbert Opel Vectra

JUNE 21 LE VIGEANT
1 Eric Cayrolle BMW 320i
2 Marcel Tarres Audi 80
3 James Ruffier Opel Vectra
4 William David Peugeot 405
5 Yvan Lebon BMW 320i
6 Willy Maljean BMW 320i

1 Eric Cayrolle BMW 320i
2 Marcel Tarres Audi 80
3 William David Peugeot 405
4 Yvan Lebon BMW 320i
5 Patrick Bourguignon BMW M3
6 Michel Quagliozzi Honda Civic

JULY 19 PAUL RICARD
1 Eric Cayrolle BMW 320i
2 William David Peugeot 405
3 Christophe Dechavanne Audi 80
4 Bruno Hernandez BMW 320i
5 Patrick Herbert Opel Vectra
6 Yvan Lebon BMW 320i

1 Eric Cayrolle BMW 320i
2 William David Peugeot 405
3 Bruno Hernandez BMW 320i
4 Patrick Herbert Opel Vectra
5 Willy Maljean BMW 320i
6 Patrick Bourguignon BMW M3

SEPTEMBER 20 LE MANS
1 Eric Cayrolle BMW 320i
2 James Ruffier Opel Vectra
3 William David Peugeot 405
4 Gilles Duqueine BMW 320i
5 Yvan Lebon BMW 320i
6 Carlos Antunes Tavares Renault Megane

1 Eric Cayrolle BMW 320i
2 Gilles Duqueine BMW 320i
3 Sylvain Noel BMW 320i
4 Patrick Herbert Opel Vectra
5 Carlos Antunes Tavares Renault Megane
6 Patrick Bourguignon BMW M3

CHAMPIONSHIP POSITIONS
1 Eric Cayrolle 119
2 Christophe Dechavanne 98
3 Patrick Herbert 53
4 James Ruffier 46
5 Yvan Lebon 40
Marcel Tarres 40
Carlos Antunes Tavares 40

STAAT/SUTTON

German champion Cecotto

GERMAN SUPER TOURING CHAMPIONSHIP

APRIL 19 HOCKENHEIM
1 Uwe Alzen Opel Vectra
2 Manuel Reuter Opel Vectra
3 Joachim Winkelhock BMW 320i
4 Laurent Aiello Peugeot 406
5 Christian Menzel BMW 320i
6 Christian Abt Audi A4

1 Manuel Reuter Opel Vectra
2 Laurent Aiello Peugeot 406
3 Joachim Winkelhock BMW 320i
4 Michael Krumm Nissan Primera
5 Christian Abt Audi A4
6 Leopold von Bayern BMW 320i

MAY 10 NURBURGRING
1 Roland Asch Nissan Primera
2 Eric Helary Opel Vectra
3 Johnny Cecotto BMW 320i
4 Laurent Aiello Peugeot 406
5 Manuel Reuter Opel Vectra
6 Uwe Alzen Opel Vectra

1 Johnny Cecotto BMW 320i
2 Eric Helary Opel Vectra
3 Laurent Aiello Peugeot 406
4 Roland Asch Nissan Primera
5 Uwe Alzen Opel Vectra
6 Jorg van Ommen Peugeot 406

MAY 24 SACHSENRING
1 Johnny Cecotto BMW 320i
2 Christian Menzel BMW 320i
3 Laurent Aiello Peugeot 406
4 Uwe Alzen Opel Vectra
5 Gabriele Tarquini Honda Accord
6 Michael Krumm Nissan Primera

1 Johnny Cecotto BMW 320i
2 Joachim Winkelhock BMW 320i
3 Roland Asch Nissan Primera
4 Jorg van Ommen Peugeot 406
5 Gabriele Tarquini Honda Accord
6 Manuel Reuter Opel Vectra

JULY 5 NORISRING
1 Jorg van Ommen Peugeot 406
2 Uwe Alzen Opel Vectra
3 Roland Asch Nissan Primera
4 Christian Abt Audi A4
5 Gabriele Tarquini Honda Accord
6 Laurent Aiello Peugeot 406

1 Laurent Aiello Peugeot 406
2 Eric Helary Opel Vectra
3 Uwe Alzen Opel Vectra
4 Johnny Cecotto BMW 320i
5 Joachim Winkelhock BMW 320i
6 Roland Asch Nissan Primera

JULY 19 LAHR
1 Uwe Alzen Opel Vectra
2 Eric Helary Opel Vectra
3 Gabriele Tarquini Honda Accord
4 Johnny Cecotto BMW 320i
5 Alexander Burgstaller Opel Vectra
6 Roland Asch Nissan Primera

1 Gabriele Tarquini Honda Accord
2 Johnny Cecotto BMW 320i
3 Eric Helary Opel Vectra
4 Uwe Alzen Opel Vectra
5 Frank Biela Audi A4
6 Manuel Reuter Opel Vectra

AUGUST 2 WUNSTORF
1 Laurent Aiello Peugeot 406
2 Manuel Reuter Opel Vectra
3 Tom Kristensen Honda Accord
4 Jorg van Ommen Peugeot 406
5 Uwe Alzen Opel Vectra
6 Michael Krumm Nissan Primera

1 Manuel Reuter Opel Vectra
2 Uwe Alzen Opel Vectra
3 Jorg van Ommen Peugeot 406
4 Eric Helary Opel Vectra
5 Tom Kristensen Honda Accord
6 Michael Krumm Nissan Primera

AUGUST 16 ZWEIBRUCKEN
1 Johnny Cecotto BMW 320i
2 Joachim Winkelhock BMW 320i
3 Laurent Aiello Peugeot 406
4 Gabriele Tarquini Honda Accord
5 Manuel Reuter Opel Vectra
6 Roland Asch Nissan Primera

1 Johnny Cecotto BMW 320i
2 Joachim Winkelhock BMW 320i
3 Roland Asch Nissan Primera
4 Eric Helary Opel Vectra
5 Laurent Aiello Peugeot 406
6 Uwe Alzen Opel Vectra

AUGUST 30 SALZBURGRING
1 Laurent Aiello Peugeot 406
2 Uwe Alzen Opel Vectra
3 Manuel Reuter Opel Vectra
4 Christian Abt Audi A4
5 Gabriele Tarquini Honda Accord
6 Jorg van Ommen Peugeot 406

1 Laurent Aiello Peugeot 406
2 Emanuele Pirro Audi A4
3 Michael Bartels Peugeot 406
4 Gabriele Tarquini Honda Accord
5 Jorg van Ommen Peugeot 406
6 Michael Krumm Nissan Primera

SEPTEMBER 13 OSCHERSLEBEN
1 Laurent Aiello Peugeot 406
2 Michael Krumm Nissan Primera
3 Johnny Cecotto BMW 320i
4 Joachim Winkelhock BMW 320i
5 Uwe Alzen Opel Vectra
6 Christian Abt Audi A4

1 Laurent Aiello Peugeot 406
2 Johnny Cecotto BMW 320i
3 Joachim Winkelhock BMW 320i
4 Michael Krumm Nissan Primera
5 Uwe Alzen Opel Vectra
6 Eric Helary Opel Vectra

OCTOBER 4 NURBURGRING
1 Manuel Reuter Opel Vectra
2 Eric Helary Opel Vectra
3 Laurent Aiello Peugeot 406
4 Johnny Cecotto BMW 320i
5 Uwe Alzen Opel Vectra
6 Frank Biela Audi A4

1 Eric Helary Opel Vectra
2 Uwe Alzen Opel Vectra
3 Manuel Reuter Opel Vectra
4 Johnny Cecotto BMW 320i
5 Tom Kristensen Honda Accord
6 Laurent Aiello Peugeot 406

CHAMPIONSHIP POSITIONS
1 Johnny Cecotto 595
2 Laurent Aiello 592
3 Uwe Alzen 482
4 Eric Helary 473
5 Manuel Reuter 423
6 Joachim Winkelhock 405

SIGNORI/SUTTON

Italian champion Giovanardi

ITALIAN SUPER TOURING CHAMPIONSHIP

MAY 17 BINETTO
1 Fabrizio de Simone BMW 320i
2 Emanuele Naspetti BMW 320i
3 Fabrizio Giovanardi Alfa Romeo 156
4 Fabian Peroni Audi A4
5 Nicola Larini Alfa Romeo 156
6 Rinaldo Capello Audi A4

1 Emanuele Naspetti BMW 320i
2 Fabrizio Giovanardi Alfa Romeo 156
3 Nicola Larini Alfa Romeo 156
4 Rinaldo Capello Audi A4
5 Christian Pescatori Alfa Romeo 155
6 Moreno Soli Audi A4

MAY 31 IMOLA
1 Fabrizio Giovanardi Alfa Romeo 156
2 Fabrizio de Simone BMW 320i
3 Emanuele Naspetti BMW 320i
4 Nicola Larini Alfa Romeo 156
5 Sandro Sardelli BMW 320i
6 Rinaldo Capello Audi A4

1 Fabrizio de Simone BMW 320i
2 Emanuele Naspetti BMW 320i
3 Fabrizio Giovanardi Alfa Romeo 156
4 Nicola Larini Alfa Romeo 156
5 Rinaldo Capello Audi A4
6 Sandro Sardelli BMW 320i

JUNE 28 MONZA
1 Nicola Larini Alfa Romeo 156
2 Rinaldo Capello Audi A4
3 Fabrizio Giovanardi Alfa Romeo 156
4 Fabrizio de Simone BMW 320i
5 Fabian Peroni Audi A4
6 Massimo Pigoli Honda Accord

1 Fabrizio Giovanardi Alfa Romeo 156
2 Nicola Larini Alfa Romeo 156
3 Rinaldo Capello Audi A4
4 Emanuele Naspetti BMW 320i
5 Fabian Peroni Audi A4
6 Miguel Ramos BMW 320i

JULY 12 VARANO
1 Emanuele Naspetti BMW 320i
2 Fabrizio de Simone BMW 320i
3 Nicola Larini Alfa Romeo 156
4 Fabian Peroni Audi A4
5 Fabrizio Giovanardi Alfa Romeo 156
6 Rinaldo Capello Audi A4

1 Emanuele Naspetti BMW 320i
2 Fabrizio Giovanardi Alfa Romeo 156
3 Nicola Larini Alfa Romeo 156
4 Fabian Peroni Audi A4
5 Rinaldo Capello Audi A4
6 Miguel Ramos BMW 320i

JULY 26 VALLELUNGA
1 Emanuele Naspetti BMW 320i
2 Fabrizio Giovanardi Alfa Romeo 156
3 Fabrizio de Simone BMW 320i
4 Nicola Larini Alfa Romeo 156
5 Rinaldo Capello Audi A4
6 Sandro Sardelli BMW 320i

1 Emanuele Naspetti BMW 320i
2 Rinaldo Capello Audi A4
3 Sandro Sardelli BMW 320i
4 Miguel Ramos BMW 320i
5 Emanuele Moncini Alfa Romeo 155
6 Moreno Soli Audi A4

Daily motorsport news on the web

www.autosportmag.com

Designed by

racecar
design

01483 203781

Powered by

INTENSIVE
NETWORKS

01672 511388

GET AHEAD OF THE PACK

26 issues for only £49.
SAVE a massive 52p an issue
Call the crdit card hotline: ☎ 01795 414817

Simply complete and return the form below, photocopies are accepted, to the address given. NO STAMP REQUIRED!

AUTOSPORT Subscription Form

☐ Please start my 26 issue subscription to Autosport, quarterly direct debit for **ONLY £49**

Must be completed: Your details
(BLOCK CAPS PLEASE)
Mr/Mrs/Miss:.....................................Initial:........................Surname:...
Address:...
....Postcode..TEL NO:...

☐ I enclose a cheque payable to **Haymarket Publishing Ltd**
☐ Please debit my
Mastercard/Visa/AMEX/Connect ☐☐☐☐☐☐☐☐☐☐☐☐☐☐☐☐☐☐☐☐☐☐☐

Valid from ☐☐/☐☐   Expiry date ☐☐/☐☐   Issue no. ☐☐ (Switch only)

Signature(s)...Date...
Just send this coupon with payment details to :
AUTOSPORT, FREEPOST SEA4876, Sittingbourne, Kent, ME9 8NR. Offer available to UK subscribers only. Overseas rates available on request by calling
01795 414 817. Offer closes on December 30th 1999. Allow 28 days for receipt of your first copy.
☐ Please tick here if you do not wish to receive further information from other carefully selected other companies.

GP128DP

AUTOSPORT
First with motor racing news, analysis, comment and features.

MONEY BACK GUARANTEE
If you decide to cancel your subscription to AUTOSPORT at any time, we will guarantee to refund the un-expired portion of your subscription.
NO QUESTIONS ASKED!

INTERNATIONAL RESULTS

AUGUST 2 — MAGIONE
1 Fabrizio Giovanardi — Alfa Romeo 156
2 Nicola Larini — Alfa Romeo 156
3 Emanuele Naspetti — BMW 320i
4 Fabrizio de Simone — BMW 320i
5 Moreno Soli — Audi A4
6 Emanuele Moncini — Alfa Romeo 155

1 Fabrizio de Simone — BMW 320i
2 Fabrizio Giovanardi — Alfa Romeo 156
3 Fabian Peroni — Audi A4
4 Rinaldo Capello — Audi A4
5 Moreno Soli — Audi A4
6 Davide Bernasconi — Audi A4

AUGUST 30 — ENNA-PERGUSA
1 Fabrizio Giovanardi — Alfa Romeo 156
2 Emanuele Naspetti — BMW 320i
3 Nicola Larini — Alfa Romeo 156
4 Fabrizio de Simone — BMW 320i
5 Rinaldo Capello — Audi A4
6 Christian Pescatori — Alfa Romeo 155
1 Fabrizio Giovanardi — Alfa Romeo 156
2 Nicola Larini — Alfa Romeo 156
3 Emanuele Naspetti — BMW 320i
4 Rinaldo Capello — Audi A4
5 Fabrizio de Simone — BMW 320i
6 Christian Pescatori — Alfa Romeo 155

SEPTEMBER 13 — MISANO
1 Fabrizio Giovanardi — Alfa Romeo 156
2 Nicola Larini — Alfa Romeo 156
3 Fabrizio de Simone — BMW 320i
4 Fabian Peroni — Audi A4
5 Roberto Colciago — BMW 320i
6 Christian Pescatori — Alfa Romeo 155

1 Roberto Colciago — BMW 320i
2 Fabian Peroni — Audi A4
3 Davide Bernasconi — Audi A4
4 Gianluca Roda — Alfa Romeo 155
5 Fabrizio de Simone — BMW 320i
6 Christian Pescatori — Alfa Romeo 155

SEPTEMBER 27 — MONZA
1 Fabrizio Giovanardi — Alfa Romeo 156
2 Nicola Larini — Alfa Romeo 156
3 Stefano Modena — Alfa Romeo 156
4 Emanuele Naspetti — BMW 320i
5 Antonio Tamburini — Alfa Romeo 156
6 Rinaldo Capello — Audi A4

1 Fabrizio Giovanardi — Alfa Romeo 156
2 Emanuele Naspetti — BMW 320i
3 Nicola Larini — Alfa Romeo 156
4 Stefano Modena — Alfa Romeo 156
5 Fabrizio de Simone — BMW 320i
6 Antonio Tamburini — Alfa Romeo 156

OCTOBER 4 — VALLELUNGA
1 Nicola Larini — Alfa Romeo 156
2 Roberto Colciago — BMW 320i
3 Fabrizio Giovanardi — Alfa Romeo 156
4 Rinaldo Capello — Audi A4
5 Antonio Tamburini — Alfa Romeo 156
6 Christian Pescatori — Alfa Romeo 155

1 Nicola Larini — Alfa Romeo 156
2 Roberto Colciago — BMW 320i
3 Fabrizio Giovanardi — Alfa Romeo 156
4 Sandro Sardelli — BMW 320i
5 Antonio Tamburini — Alfa Romeo 156
6 Fabian Peroni — Audi A4

CHAMPIONSHIP POSITIONS
1 Fabrizio Giovanardi — 431
2 Emanuele Naspetti — 335
3 Nicola Larini — 331
4 Fabrizio de Simone — 244
5 Rinaldo Capello — 217
6 Fabian Peroni — 177

JAPANESE TOURING CAR CHAMPIONSHIP

APRIL 5 — FUJI
1 Hironori Takeuchi — Toyota Chaser
2 Takeshi Tsuchiya — Toyota Exiv
3 Keiichi Tsuchiya — Toyota Chaser
4 Ruben Derfler — Toyota Exiv
5 Tatsuya Tanigawa — Toyota Exiv
6 Kelvin Burt — Toyota Chaser

1 Katsutomo Kaneishi — Toyota Exiv
2 Masanori Sekiya — Toyota Chaser
3 Yuji Tachikawa — Toyota Chaser
4 Kelvin Burt — Toyota Chaser
5 Takeshi Tsuchiya — Toyota Exiv
6 Hironori Takeuchi — Toyota Chaser

MAY 10 — MOTEGI
1 Masanori Sekiya — Toyota Chaser
2 Yuji Tachikawa — Toyota Chaser
3 Takeshi Tsuchiya — Toyota Exiv
4 Hironori Takeuchi — Toyota Chaser
5 Kelvin Burt — Toyota Chaser
6 Katsutomo Kaneishi — Toyota Exiv

MAY 24 — SUGO
1 Masanori Sekiya — Toyota Chaser
2 Hironori Takeuchi — Toyota Chaser
3 Katsutomo Kaneishi — Toyota Exiv

SEKINE/SUTTON
Japanese racewinner Kaneishi

4 Kelvin Burt — Toyota Chaser
5 Keiichi Tsuchiya — Toyota Chaser
6 Yuji Tachikawa — Toyota Chaser

1 Kelvin Burt — Toyota Chaser
2 Hironori Takeuchi — Toyota Chaser
3 Masanori Sekiya — Toyota Chaser
4 Yuji Tachikawa — Toyota Chaser
5 Ruben Derfler — Toyota Exiv
6 Keiichi Tsuchiya — Toyota Chaser

JUNE 21 — SUZUKA
1 Katsutomo Kaneishi — Toyota Exiv
2 Yuji Tachikawa — Toyota Chaser
3 Hironori Takeuchi — Toyota Chaser
4 Masanori Sekiya — Toyota Chaser
5 Takeshi Tsuchiya — Toyota Exiv
6 Ruben Derfler — Toyota Exiv

1 Masanori Sekiya — Toyota Chaser
2 Katsutomo Kaneishi — Toyota Exiv
3 Hironori Takeuchi — Toyota Chaser
4 Keiichi Tsuchiya — Toyota Chaser
5 Takeshi Tsuchiya — Toyota Exiv
6 Akihiko Nakaya — Toyota Exiv

JULY 26 — MINE
1 Masanori Sekiya — Toyota Chaser
2 Hironori Takeuchi — Toyota Chaser
3 Katsutomo Kaneishi — Toyota Exiv
4 Takeshi Tsuchiya — Toyota Exiv
5 Yuji Tachikawa — Toyota Chaser
6 Ruben Derfler — Toyota Exiv

1 Masanori Sekiya — Toyota Chaser
2 Katsutomo Kaneishi — Toyota Exiv
3 Yuji Tachikawa — Toyota Chaser
4 Kelvin Burt — Toyota Chaser
5 Keiichi Tsuchiya — Toyota Chaser
6 Ruben Derfler — Toyota Exiv

AUGUST 16 — TI CIRCUIT
1 Masanori Sekiya — Toyota Chaser
2 Kelvin Burt — Toyota Chaser
3 Yuji Tachikawa — Toyota Chaser
4 Keiichi Tsuchiya — Toyota Chaser
5 Ruben Derfler — Toyota Exiv
6 Takeshi Tsuchiya — Toyota Exiv

CHAMPIONSHIP POSITIONS
(with one round to go at Fuji)
1 Masanori Sekiya — 121
2 Hironori Takeuchi — 85
3 Katsutomo Kaneishi — 80
4 Yuji Tachikawa — 73
5 Kelvin Burt — 59
6 Takeshi Tsuchiya — 55

NEW ZEALAND TOURING CAR CHAMPIONSHIP

CHAMPIONSHIP POSITIONS
1 Brett Riley (BMW 320i) — 312
2 Jason Richards (BMW 320i) — 291
3 Barrie Thomlinson (Ford Telstar) — 186
4 Peter van Breugel (Nissan Sentra) — 165
5 Geoff Short (Ford Telstar) — 116
6 Mike Eady (Toyota Corolla) — 64

SOUTH AFRICAN TOURING CAR CHAMPIONSHIP

FEBRUARY 14 — KYALAMI
1 Giniel de Villiers — Nissan Primera
2 Shaun van der Linde — BMW 318i
3 Terry Moss — Audi A4
4 Duncan Vos — Nissan Primera
5 Mike Briggs — BMW 318i
6 Nico van Rensburg — Nissan Sentra

1 Chris Aberdein — Audi A4
2 Terry Moss — Audi A4
3 Marco dos Santos — Nissan Sentra
4 Duncan Vos — Nissan Primera
5 Shaun van der Linde — BMW 318i
6 Mark Peters — BMW 318i

MARCH 14 — ALDO SCRIBANTE
1 Giniel de Villiers — Nissan Primera
2 Hilton Cowie — Toyota Corolla
3 Terry Moss — Audi A4
4 Hennie Groenewald — Audi A4
5 Marco dos Santos — Nissan Sentra
6 Nico van Rensburg — Nissan Sentra

1 Duncan Vos — Nissan Primera
2 Giniel de Villiers — Nissan Primera
3 Shaun van der Linde — BMW 318i
4 Mike Briggs — BMW 318i
5 Terry Moss — Audi A4
6 Chris Aberdein — Audi A4

APRIL 4 — KILLARNEY
1 Giniel de Villiers — Nissan Primera
2 Marco dos Santos — Nissan Sentra
3 Chris Aberdein — Audi A4
4 Duncan Vos — Nissan Primera
5 Terry Moss — Audi A4
6 George Bezuidenhout — Nissan Sentra

1 Duncan Vos — Nissan Primera
2 Giniel de Villiers — Nissan Primera
3 Marco dos Santos — Nissan Sentra
4 Chris Aberdein — Audi A4
5 Terry Moss — Audi A4
6 George Bezuidenhout — Nissan Sentra

APRIL 25 — KYALAMI
1 Giniel de Villiers — Nissan Primera
2 Duncan Vos — Nissan Primera
3 Anthony Taylor — Audi A4
4 Shaun van der Linde — BMW 318i
5 Mike Briggs — BMW 318i
6 Terry Moss — Audi A4

1 Chris Aberdein — Audi A4
2 Anthony Taylor — Audi A4
3 Giniel de Villiers — Nissan Primera
4 Terry Moss — Audi A4
5 Duncan Vos — Nissan Primera
6 Marco dos Santos — Nissan Sentra

MAY 30 — GOLDFIELDS
1 Giniel de Villiers — Nissan Primera
2 Shaun van der Linde — BMW 318i
3 Chris Aberdein — Audi A4
4 Terry Moss — Audi A4
5 Duncan Vos — Nissan Primera
6 Anthony Taylor — Audi A4

1 Shaun van der Linde — BMW 318i
2 Giniel de Villiers — Nissan Primera
3 Duncan Vos — Nissan Primera
4 Mike Briggs — BMW 318i
5 Terry Moss — Audi A4
6 Chris Aberdein — Audi A4

AUGUST 8 — EAST LONDON
1 Giniel de Villiers — Nissan Primera
2 Shaun van der Linde — BMW 318i
3 Terry Moss — Audi A4
4 Chris Aberdein — Audi A4
5 Mark Peters — BMW 318i
6 Garth Waberski — Toyota Camry

1 Giniel de Villiers — Nissan Primera
2 Anthony Taylor — Audi A4
3 Mike Briggs — BMW 318i
4 Duncan Vos — Nissan Primera
5 Hilton Cowie — Toyota Corolla
6 Chris Aberdein — Audi A4

AUGUST 29 — ALDO SCRIBANTE
1 Shaun van der Linde — BMW 318i
2 Terry Moss — Audi A4
3 Giniel de Villiers — Nissan Primera
4 Duncan Vos — Nissan Primera
5 Anthony Taylor — Audi A4
6 Mark Peters — BMW 318i

1 Shaun van der Linde — BMW 318i
2 Giniel de Villiers — Nissan Primera
3 Terry Moss — Audi A4
4 Marco dos Santos — Nissan Sentra
5 Mike Briggs — BMW 318i
6 Mark Peters — BMW 318i

SEPTEMBER 26 — KYALAMI
1 Mike Briggs — BMW 318i
2 Shaun van der Linde — BMW 318i
3 Marco dos Santos — Nissan Sentra
4 Mark Peters — BMW 318i
5 Garth Waberski — Toyota Camry
6 George Bezuidenhout — Nissan Sentra

1 Shaun van der Linde — BMW 318i
2 Giniel de Villiers — Nissan Primera
3 Mike Briggs — BMW 318i
4 Terry Moss — Audi A4
5 Marco dos Santos — Nissan Sentra
6 Anthony Taylor — Audi A4

CHAMPIONSHIP POSITIONS
(with rounds to go at Killarney & Kyalami)
1 Giniel de Villiers — 212
2 Shaun van der Linde — 151
3 Duncan Vos — 131
4 Terry Moss — 126
5 Chris Aberdein — 96
6 Mike Briggs — 83

SOUTH AMERICAN TOURING CAR CHAMPIONSHIP

MARCH 22 — BUENOS AIRES
1 Oscar Larrauri — BMW 320i
2 Ernesto Bessone — Chrysler Stratus
3 Osvaldo Lopez — Alfa Romeo 155
4 Miguel Angel Guerra — Chevrolet Vectra
5 Paulo Gomes — Chevrolet Vectra
6 Ricardo Risatti — Ford Mondeo

APRIL 12 — BUENOS AIRES
1 Oscar Larrauri — BMW 320i
2 Carlos Bueno — Peugeot 406
3 Ernesto Bessone — Chrysler Stratus
4 Ingo Hoffmann — BMW 320i
5 Fernando Croceri — BMW 320i
6 Juan Manuel Fangio II — Peugeot 406

MAY 17 — LONDRINA
1 Carlos Bueno — Peugeot 406
2 Osvaldo Lopez — Alfa Romeo 155
3 Ingo Hoffmann — BMW 320i
4 Emiliano Spataro — Chevrolet Vectra
5 Javier Balzano — Chevrolet Vectra
6 Miguel Angel Guerra — Chevrolet Vectra

JULY 5 — POSADAS
1 Oscar Larrauri — BMW 320i
2 Juan Manuel Fangio II — Peugeot 406
3 Carlos Bueno — Peugeot 406
4 Fernando Croceri — BMW 320i
5 Oscar Fineschi — Toyota Corona
6 Ricardo Risatti — Ford Mondeo

JULY 26 — MAR DE AJO
1 Oscar Larrauri — BMW 320i
2 Carlos Bueno — Peugeot 406
3 Juan Manuel Fangio II — Peugeot 406
4 Osvaldo Lopez — Alfa Romeo 155
5 Ingo Hoffmann — BMW 320i
6 Pablo Peon — Chrysler Stratus

AUGUST 2 — OLAVARRIA
1 Juan Manuel Fangio II — Peugeot 406
2 Osvaldo Lopez — Alfa Romeo 155
3 Carlos Bueno — Peugeot 406
4 Emiliano Spataro — Alfa Romeo 155
5 Miguel Angel Guerra — Chevrolet Vectra
6 Pablo Peon — Chrysler Stratus

AUGUST 23 — CURITIBA
1 Ingo Hoffmann — BMW 320i
2 Osvaldo Lopez — Alfa Romeo 155
3 Emiliano Spataro — Alfa Romeo 155
4 Miguel Angel Guerra — Chevrolet Vectra
5 Juan Manuel Fangio II — Peugeot 406
6 Ernesto Bessone — Chrysler Stratus

SEPTEMBER 6 — OBERA
1 Ingo Hoffmann — BMW 320i
2 Oscar Larrauri — BMW 320i
3 Juan Manuel Fangio II — Peugeot 406
4 Fernando Croceri — BMW 320i
5 Osvaldo Lopez — Alfa Romeo 155
6 Carlos Bueno — Peugeot 406

OCTOBER 4 — BUENOS AIRES
1 Oscar Larrauri — BMW 320i
2 Oscar Fineschi — Toyota Corona
3 Ernesto Bessone — Chrysler Stratus
4 Carlos Bueno — Peugeot 406
5 Osvaldo Lopez — Alfa Romeo 155
6 Juan Manuel Fangio II — Peugeot 406

CHAMPIONSHIP POSITIONS
(with rounds to go at Goiania, Montevideo & Interlagos)
1 Oscar Larrauri — 118
2 Carlos Bueno — 98
3 Osvaldo Lopez — 83
4 Juan Manuel Fangio II — 79
5 Ingo Hoffmann — 75
6 Ernesto Bessone — 46

DECURNEX/SUTTON
SudAm champion Larrauri

SWEDISH SUPER TOURING CHAMPIONSHIP

MAY 10 — MANTORP PARK
1 Mats Linden — Audi A4
2 Jan Brunstedt — Opel Vectra
3 Carl Rosenblad — Nissan Primera
4 Fredrik Ekblom — BMW 318i
5 Tommy Kristofersson — Audi A4
6 Richard Goranson — Ford Mondeo

1 Fredrik Ekblom — BMW 318i
2 Mats Linden — Audi A4
3 Tommy Kristofersson — Audi A4
4 Per-Gunnar Andersson — BMW 318i
5 Carl Rosenblad — Nissan Primera
6 Jan Brunstedt — Opel Vectra

MAY 31 — KARLSKOGA
1 Jan Nilsson — Volvo S40
2 Fredrik Ekblom — BMW 318i
3 Mattias Ekstrom — Ford Mondeo
4 Per-Gunnar Andersson — BMW 318i
5 Pontus Morth — Opel Vectra
6 Tommy Kristofersson — Audi A4

1 Per-Gunnar Andersson — BMW 318i
2 Fredrik Ekblom — BMW 318i
3 Mats Linden — Audi A4
4 Jan Nilsson — Volvo S40
5 Pontus Morth — Opel Vectra
6 Jan Brunstedt — Opel Vectra

JUNE 28 — ANDERSTORP
1 Jan Nilsson — Volvo S40
2 Mattias Ekstrom — Ford Mondeo
3 Fredrik Ekblom — BMW 318i
4 Mats Linden — Audi A4
5 Thomas Johansson — Opel Vectra
6 Pontus Morth — Opel Vectra

1 Per-Gunnar Andersson — BMW 318i
2 Jan Nilsson — Volvo S40
3 Mattias Ekstrom — Ford Mondeo
4 Fredrik Ekblom — BMW 318i
5 Carl Rosenblad — Nissan Primera
6 Tommy Kristofersson — Audi A4

AUGUST 9 — FALKENBERG
1 Jan Nilsson — Volvo S40
2 Jens Edman — Volvo S40
3 Jan Brunstedt — Opel Vectra
4 Pontus Morth — Opel Vectra
5 Carl Rosenblad — Nissan Primera
6 Kari Makinen — Nissan Primera

1 Jens Edman — Volvo S40
2 Fredrik Ekblom — BMW 318i
3 Jan Brunstedt — Opel Vectra
4 Mats Linden — Audi A4
5 Pontus Morth — Opel Vectra
6 Kari Makinen — Nissan Primera

SEPTEMBER 6 — KNUTSTORP
1 Fredrik Ekblom — BMW 318i
2 Per-Gunnar Andersson — BMW 318i
3 Mats Linden — Audi A4
4 Mattias Ekstrom — Ford Mondeo
5 Jan Nilsson — Volvo S40
6 Jens Edman — Volvo S40

1 Jan Nilsson — Volvo S40
2 Mattias Ekstrom — Ford Mondeo
3 Fredrik Ekblom — BMW 318i
4 Thomas Johansson — Opel Vectra
5 Per-Gunnar Andersson — BMW 318i
6 Tommy Kristofersson — Audi A4

SEPTEMBER 27 — MANTORP PARK
1 Fredrik Ekblom — BMW 318i
2 Tommy Kristofersson — Audi A4
3 Jan Nilsson — Volvo S40
4 Per-Gunnar Andersson — BMW 318i
5 Jens Edman — Volvo S40
6 Jan Brunstedt — Opel Vectra

1 Jan Nilsson — Volvo S40
2 Fredrik Ekblom — BMW 318i
3 Tommy Kristofersson — Audi A4
4 Stefan Lindberg — Honda Accord
5 Jan Brunstedt — Opel Vectra
6 Carl Rosenblad — Nissan Primera

CHAMPIONSHIP POSITIONS
1 Fredrik Ekblom — 229
2 Jan Nilsson — 207
3 Per-Gunnar Andersson — 137
4 Tommy Kristofersson — 128
5 Mats Linden — 115
6 Jan Brunstedt — 114

OTHER TOURING CAR RACES

MARCH 6-8 — MELBOURNE
AUSTRALIAN GP SUPPORTS
1 Russell Ingall — Holden Commodore
2 Mark Skaife — Holden Commodore
3 John Bowe — Ford Falcon
4 Tony Longhurst — Ford Falcon
5 Jason Bright — Ford Falcon
6 Glenn Seton — Ford Falcon

1 Russell Ingall — Holden Commodore
2 John Bowe — Ford Falcon
3 Mark Skaife — Holden Commodore
4 Larry Perkins — Holden Commodore
5 Glenn Seton — Ford Falcon
6 Dick Johnson — Ford Falcon

1 Russell Ingall — Holden Commodore
2 John Bowe — Ford Falcon
3 Mark Skaife — Holden Commodore
4 Larry Perkins — Holden Commodore
5 Glenn Seton — Ford Falcon
6 Dick Johnson — Ford Falcon

OCTOBER 4 — BATHURST
AMP BATHURST 1000
1 Rickard Rydell/Jim Richards — Volvo S40
2 Steven Richards/Matt Neal — Nissan Primera
3 Brad Jones/Cam McConville — Audi A4
4 Cameron McLean/Tony Scott — BMW 320i
5 John Cleland/Derek Warwick — Vauxhall Vectra
6 Peter Hills/Domenic Beninca — Ford Mondeo
7 Troy Searle/Luke Searle — BMW 320i
8 Rod Wilson/Rodney Forbes — BMW 318i
9 Bob Holden/Jim Matthews/Paul Nelson — BMW 320i
10 Kevin Bell/Rod Hicks — BMW 320i

UP FOR THE CUP

SEE YOU NEXT YEAR